THE BOOK OF THE

Hastings International Masters' Chess Tournament

1922

CONTAINING ALL THE GAMES PLAYED
WITH ANNOTATIONS BY THE WINNER,

A. ALEKHINE

AND AN ACCOUNT OF THE TOURNAMENT BY
SIR G. A. THOMAS (BART.)

Edited by

W. H. Watts

DOVER PUBLICATIONS, INC., NEW YORK

This Dover edition, first published in 1968, is an unabridged republication of the work printed in 1923 by Printing Craft Ltd., London.

International Standard Book Number: 0-486-21960-7
Library of Congress Catalog Card Number: 68-12912

Manufactured in the United States of America
Dover Publications, Inc.
180 Varick Street
New York, N.Y. 10014

PREFACE

Despite perhaps the most capricious career that any Chess Manuscript has ever had, Alekhine's Annotations to the games played in the Hastings Tournament of 1922 are at last published.

It is mainly due to Alekhine that the games are now published in this country, for readers will, I think, agree that his work has been most thoroughly and conscientiously carried out, and the book constitutes almost a record in Chess annotation. It was because this exhaustive and critical examination of the games was so complete and so intensely interesting, that it was finally decided to publish despite the long delay. A second reason was the general high quality of the games themselves. As an instance—the game in the second round between Sir G. A. Thomas and Rubinstein runs to 114 moves, but positions of interest occur every few moves right to the end. After Rubinstein missed his first winning line of play, thrust and counter-thrust mark every few moves, and even at the finish, when the players were practically compelled to abandon the game as a draw, it is necessary for Alekhine to add a note explaining how the draw is secured. Almost all the other games are equally interesting. In addition to Alekhine's notes a few from " The Field " and a few original ones have been added.

Regarding the delay :—As General Editor, I claim for myself absolution and hope to be pardoned for not going into the question of responsibility. Suffice it to say that in my opinion there must have been a misunderstanding between the parties concerned.

My only remaining duty is a very pleasing one, and that is to render this small expression of thanks to Mr. P. G. Asbury, of London, an old Chess playing friend, for his able translation of more than half of the manuscript; Mr. A. H. E. Johnson, of New Brighton, for his painstaking checking of proofs and general assistance whilst the book was in the press; and to Mr. E. J. Ackroyd, the Tournament Secretary, whose affable and tractable nature is already known to the Chess World at large. Without him there would have been no book, but had we been favoured by his uninterrupted help publication would have been effected long ago.

W. H. WATTS.

April, 1924.

" The words Black and White have been omitted from the tops of the columns as they are considered unnecessary, and I would specially advise readers to plainly mark their Knights and Rooks so that they can readily identify the K Kt from the Q Kt and the K R from the Q R."

TABLE OF OPENINGS

Numbers refer to Games.

TABLE OF GAMES AND PLAYERS

The numbers refer to pages.

		playing black				
	1	2	3	4	5	6
1 Alekhine		38	57	46	18	28
2 Rubinstein	15		44	59	32	26
3 Bogoljubow	57	19		29	50	39
4 Thomas	22	37	52		40	43
5 Tarrasch	41	55	25	13		35
6 Yates	55	52	21	25	66	

playing white

TABLE OF CONTENTS

THE HASTINGS INTERNATIONAL MASTERS' CHESS TOURNAMENT, 1922

INTRODUCTION, by SIR G. A. THOMAS (Bart.)

The town of Hastings has taken a very prominent part in British chess affairs during the last thirty years or so; but, even in so fine a record, the Invitation Tournament held in September, 1922, stands out as an event of exceptional interest and importance.

Among other noteworthy features was the fact that the tournament was officially organized by the local municipality—quite a new departure in such affairs, so far as this country is concerned. On the continent it is, of course, a very ordinary incident in chess enterprise; and that is one reason why the continental master has so many more opportunities for constant first-rate practice than our home players. I believe the Hastings Council were well satisfied with the practical results of the Tournament, from the point of view of benefit to the town; which shows that enterprise of this sort may be of use in other ways besides the development of chess; and if this encouraging result should induce other local bodies to follow the lead given by Hastings, the gain to British Chess will be incalculable. We undoubtedly have, in the British Isles, a large number of players possessing natural talent of a very high order, and capable, given facilities for acquiring the necessary experience, of holding their own in any company, but few of these will ever do themselves complete justice until they are provided with much more frequent opportunities for serious tournament practice than is at present the case.

While directly under the auspices of the municipality, the actual working of the Tournament was, naturally, largely in the hands of leading members of the Hastings Chess Club—particularly Mr. H. E. Dobell the president, and himself a member of the local Council, the late Mr. H. F. Cheshire, and Mr. E. J. Ackroyd (the congress honorary secretary); and no one who has experienced their ability in organization need be told that the arrangements were admirable, down to the smallest detail. The Mayor (Alderman W. J. Fellowes) also did much more than give official support to the Tournament, working throughout with keen interest. In fact, the management could not have been bettered, everything possible being done for the comfort of the players.

One of the conditions of play calling for special reference was the time-limit—17 moves an hour as against the 20 usual in British tournaments. I wish other of our tournaments would adopt a slower rate. In my opinion, 20 moves an hour is altogether too fast for the best type of play; and I think its general adoption among us is largely responsible for the lack of depth in so many of our tournament games. Abroad, in serious chess, the recognized rate is 15 moves an hour; and until we come into line with this I am sure our representatives will be handicapped in International contests, for, when playing at a rate slower than that to which one is accustomed, it is hardly possible to make the best use of the extra time at one's disposal. I may point out here that the City of London Chess Club reduced the rate for its Championship Tournament, from 20 to 18 moves an hour, a couple of years ago; and I am confident it would improve British Chess if this were done at other Congresses. It is a point on which I hold a very strong view.

The tournament was a double round affair, with six players; and the continental competitors were a very formidable contingent—A. Alekhine, A. Rubinstein, E. D. Bogoljubow and Dr. S. Tarrasch. The records of these famous players are already so well known that I will say no more here than that it would scarcely have been possible to gather together a more representative quartette, or one better illustrative of the wide differences of style obtaining among the greatest experts. The entry was completed by F. D. Yates, the holder for the fourth time of the British Championship—who had already proved his worth in more than one international contest—and myself.

In the result, Alekhine added one more to his many triumphs. His victory was, I think, in accordance with popular expectation; and was certainly entirely justified on the run of the play, though he actually finished only half-a-point ahead of Rubinstein. In spite of his enterprising and adventurous methods, he gave his opponents few opportunities; and the balance of luck did not in any way favour him. He produced some remarkably fine games, distinguished equally by depth and originality, and worthy of inclusion in any collection.

Rubinstein came in second, but his performance was more unequal than Alekhine's. In his better games he played beautiful chess, showing all the masterly judgment and perfect technique for which he is so famous. Nevertheless on two or three occasions he fell below his normal standard; and but for one or two strokes of good fortune—notably against Bogoljubow—he would hardly have been in the position of having a chance, up to the very last round, of tieing for first place.

There is, I think, nothing special to say here of the other competitors; except that Yates was, unfortunately, in poor health at the time—this being the cause of his disappointing score. That this had no relation to his real merit he proved, in brilliant style, a few months later at Carlsbad, where he accomplished the finest performance achieved by an English player in International Chess since the retirement of Burn and Blackburne.

Taken as a whole, the games form, I think, a fine collection. But there were one or two curious lapses. In my first game against Bogoljubow, for example, we agreed to a draw—after a very fluctuating struggle—in a position 'where Bogoljubow had a perfectly simple win. I was no more aware of it than my opponent; but I have never witnessed a more spontaneous unanimity of purpose than that with which the other continental players invaded our board, the instant the draw was accepted. to demonstrate to Bogoljubow the extreme simplicity of the winning method!

Another humorous incident arose from the inordinate length of my game with Rubinstein in the final round. Curiously enough, the destination of every prize depended on the result of this game. But when the appointed hour for the final ceremony arrived we were still hard at it. The Mayoress, who was to distribute the prizes, went for a walk—and returned to find us still battling merrily (?) on. Rumour has it that she took a second walk—and then (as the saying goes) *some*! Anyhow, it was only after, I think, fourteen hours' play that we reached a decision and enabled the belated *finale* to be staged.

GENERAL ACCOUNT OF
THE TOURNAMENT

During the early days of the London International Tournament of 1922 it was rumoured that the energetic Hastings Club were organising a Masters' Tournament. It was hoped that the participation of both Capablanca and Lasker would be secured, but first one and then the other dropped out for reasons it is unnecessary to go into here.

Eventually it was decided to make the event a double round Tournament of six players. Four of the London competitors, with Dr. Tarrasch and the welcome inclusion of Sir G. A. Thomas as a second English representative, made up the list of contestants, and the tourney started on September 10th and finished on September 21st.

It was organised by the municipality of Hastings, mainly through the zeal of the Mayor, Alderman W. J. Fellowes. Unfortunately he was unable to be present on the opening occasion, and the official welcome was therefore given by the Deputy Mayor, Alderman E. C. Smith, who, with Councillor H. E. Dobell, the well-known President of the Hastings Chess Club, also contributed largely to the success of the event. Appreciative mention should also be made of the generous help of Sir Henry Lunn, who accommodated the players at the Albany Hotel, and Mr. J. A. Watt, of the Waverley Hotel, who rendered similar service.

The Council Chamber, where the play took place, is a handsome room, and the quiet necessary to match play was effectively maintained by the excellent plan of having the moves repeated on demonstration boards in an adjoining room, where discussion on the games proceeding could be made without disturbing the players. This section was under the able management of the late Mr. H. F. Cheshire, who took a special delight in explaining the games to visitors.

Following is a complete score table showing result of each encounter distinctly, and also enabling the reader at a glance to tell which player had the move in any game.

Sir George Thomas kindly consented to write an account of the Tournament, so that a few general remarks will suffice as a survey of the event.

Many of the games will stand for all time as fine examples of chess, especially Thomas v. Rubinstein and Bogoljubow v. Alekhine. The fact that the time limit was 17 moves an hour did not prevent competitors getting short of time, nor were there fewer blunders, and it certainly meant a greater number of adjournments than a time limit of 20 moves.

Undoubtedly Alekhine's enterprising play will always make him a favourite with chess players. Rubinstein at times is just as enterprising. Bogoljubow played some bright games, but seems a little more uneven in his play than the first two prize-winners. Sir George Thomas played sufficiently well to uphold the credit of British Chess, but it is quite obvious from the opportunities that he missed that he, with our other leading players, requires more practice against the best continental players.

Dr. Tarrasch, although getting on in years, is still a difficult man to beat, but *anno domini* is bound to tell in long games.

The reason for Yates's poor score was evidently his state of health and the fact that he was also reporting at the same time. It was apparent that he had not recovered from the strain of the London Congress.

There was a good attendance of spectators throughout the tourney who thoroughly enjoyed the sporting games in which most of the players indulged.

The general arrangements and organisation of the Tournament were in the capable hands of Mr. E. J. Ackroyd, who carried the Tournament through from start to finish in the true Hastings manner, to the complete satisfaction of the competitors and visitors, the Hastings Chess Club, and last, but not least by any means, the Hastings Corporation.

No.	Name.	A. Alekhine	A. Rubinstein.	E. D. Bogoljubow.	Sir G. A. Thomas	Dr. S. Tarrasch	F. D. Yates.	Round Scores.	Total Score.
1.	A. Alekhine		B. 1 W. ½	W.1 B. 1	B. 1 W.1	W. 1 B. ½	W. 0 B. ½	4 3½	7½
2.	A. Rubinstein	W. 0 B. ½		B. 1 W. 1	B. 1 W. ½	W. 1 B. ½	W. ½ B. 1	3½ 3½	7
3.	E. D. Bogoljubow	B. 0 W. 0	W. 0 B. 0		W. ½ B. ½	B. ½ W. 1	B. 1 W. 1	2 2½	4½
4.	Sir G. A Thomas	W. 0 B. 0	W. 0 B. ½	B. ½ W. ½		B. ½ W. ½	B. 1 W. 1	2 2½	4½
5.	Dr. S. Tarrasch	B. 0 W. ½	B. 0 W. ½	W. ½ B. 0	W. ½ B. ½		W. 1 B. ½	2 2	4
6.	F. D. Yates	B. 1 W. ½	B. ½ W. 0	W. 0 B. 0	W. 0 B. 0	B. 0 W. ½		1½ 1	2½

Alexander Alekhine, first with a score of 7 ½.

Akiba Rubinstein, second with a score of 7.

E. D. BOGOLJUBOW, equal third and fourth with a score of $4\frac{1}{2}$.

SIR G. A. THOMAS (BART.), equal third and fourth with a score of $4\frac{1}{2}$.

DR. S. TARRASCH, fifth with a score of 4.

F. D. YATES, sixth with a score of $2\frac{1}{2}$.

Hastings International Congress

ROUND I

Game 1. TARRASCH *v.* THOMAS.

Queen's Gambit Declined.

TARRASCH	THOMAS	TARRASCH	THOMAS
1 P—Q 4	Kt—K B 3	36 R×P (20)	R×R (21)
2 Kt—K B 3	P—Q 4	37 Q×R	Q×P ch
3 P—B 4	P—K 3	38 Q×Q	R×Q
4 Kt—B 3	Q Kt—Q 2	39 K—B 2	R—K 2
5 B—Kt 5	B—K 2	40 P—Kt 5	K—Kt 2
6 P—K 3	O—O	41 Kt—Q 3 (22)	B—K 3
7 R—B 1	P—B 3	42 Kt—K 5	B—Q 4
8 Q—B 2	R—K 1	43 R—B 3	P—Q R 4 (23)
9 P×P (1)	Kt×P	44 P—K Kt 3	P—R 5
10 B×B (2)	Q×B	45 K—K 3	R—K 1 (24)
11 B—K 2 (3)	Kt×Kt	46 K—Q 2	R—K B 1
12 Q×Kt	P—K 4 (4)	47 Kt—Q 3 (25)	R—B 4
13 O—O	P—K 5 (5)	48 Kt—B 4	R×P
14 Kt—Q 2	Kt—Kt 3	49 Kt×B	R×Kt
15 Q—B 5	Q—R 5 (6)	50 R—B 4	R—Q R 4
16 K R—K 1 (7)	Kt—Q 4 (8)	51 R—Kt 4 (26)	P—Kt 4
17 B—B 4	B—K 3	52 P—Q 5 (27)	P—B 4
18 P—Q R 3 (9)	P—Q R 3 (10)	53 R—K 4 (28)	R—R 2 (29)
19 Q—Q 6	P—K B 4	54 R—K 6	R—Q 2
20 Q—Kt 3 (11)	Q—B 3	55 P—Q 6	K—B 2
21 Kt—Kt 3	Q R—Q 1	56 R—R 6	K—K 1
22 Kt—B 5	B—B 1		
23 P—Q R 4 (12)	K—R 1		
24 B×Kt	R×B	Position after 28.., Q—Q 1.
25 P—R 5	P—B 5 (13)	
26 Q×P	R—B 4	
27 Q—B 7	Q—R 5	
28 Q—Kt 3	Q—Q 1	

(see diagram)

29 P—R 3 (14)	Q×R P
30 Q—R 4	P—K Kt 4 (15)
31 Q—R 5	Q—Q 1
32 Q—K 2 (16)	R—B 2 (17)
33 R—B 1	P—Kt 5 (18)
34 P×P	Q—Kt 4
35 P—B 3 (19)	P×P

57 K—B 2	R—Q 1	67 R—Kt 6 ch	K—Kt 4
58 R—R 5 (30)	R×P	68 R—Kt 5 ch	K—R 5
59 R×B P	R—Q Kt 3	69 K—K 1	R—K B 5
60 R—B 7	P—R 3	70 P—Kt 3	P—R 6
61 K—Kt 1	R—Kt 3	71 R—R 5	R—B 6 (32)
62 R—Q Kt 7	R—Kt 4	72 R×P	K—Kt 6
63 P—K Kt 4 (31)	R×P	73 R—R 5	P—R 5
64 R×P	K—B 2	74 R—Kt 5 ch	K—B 4
65 K—B 2	K—Kt 3	75 R—Kt 8	
66 K—Q 2	P—R 4		Drawn (33)

(1) A serious waste of time which allows Black to equalise the game. In my opinion the correct continuation is as follows : 9 B—Q 3, P×P ; 10 B×P, Kt—Q 4 ; 11 Kt—K 4 ! as in my game against Yates in London.

(2) Exchanging the Bishops frees Black's game. If 10 B—K B 4, Kt×B and the resulting doubled Pawn would be advantageous to White.

(3) It is not clear why this Bishop is not developed on the more aggressive square B 4. White plays the initial part of this game limply.

(4) The freeing move in this position after which Black has nothing further to fear.

(5) This move divides the board strategically into two entities : Black foreshadows a King's side attack whilst White has some chances of initiative on the Queen's side.

(6) It is easily understandable that Black seeks to avoid an exchange of Queens which would nullify his chances of attack.

(7) In order to counter the menace of R—K 3, followed by R—R 3, by Kt—B 1, White might however await this contingency.

(8) This appears to me a trifle premature ; more important would have been the mobilisation of the Queen's side forces by 16.., B—Kt 5 followed by Q R—Q 1

(9) So that the Knight should not even dream of reaching Q 6. by way of Q Kt 5. White plays warily—perhaps too much so !

(10) This seems also weak and creates a relative weakness on the Queen's side. P—B 4 at once was indicated.

(11) By this means White holds back the attack and uses the respite to reinforce the Queen's side.

(12) Making use of Black's weak 18th move to maintain the Knight in its dominating position.

(13) Very ingenious but not quite correct ; it is understandable, however, that Black should seek complications previous to White obtaining a superiority on the Queen's side by 26 P—Kt 4, etc.

(14) A timid move, allowing Black to regain the sacrificed Pawn whilst retaining the attack. White could and should have played here : 29 P—Kt 4, if now 29.., R—Kt 4 ; 30 Q—B 4 !, R—B 4 (or 30.., B—R 6 ; 31 P—Kt 3 or 30.., R—B 1 ; 31 Q×P always with an adequate defence) ; 31 Q—Kt 8 ! and White can in all cases ward off the attack owing to the action of the pin by the White Queen. Through his last move White's inferiority becomes more and more pronounced.

(15) Not merely the only move to save the King's Pawn but the beginning of an attack on the weakened King's position through 29 P—R 3. From here on to the position where the game should have been won Black plays with great vigour.

(16) Black was threatening 32.., P—Kt 5, etc.

(17) A subtle move preparing the final stroke.

(18) Decisive.

(19) Evidently the only defence to 35.., B×P followed by 36.., R—B 6.

(20) After 36 P×P, R×K P followed by 37.., P—K R 4 and White's King's side is untenable. The text-move is a sheer piece of bluff which is lucky enough to succeed.

(21) It is truly extraordinary that Sir George Thomas who has so far played this game clearly and well should have omitted to see that 36.., B×P wins at once, as White cannot answer with 37 R—Kt 3 (as might have been intended on account of 37.., Q×Kt winning a clear piece. Black's last move leads to a difficult end-game with only a slight advantage.

(22) White still has a difficult game owing to the weakness of the Pawns, perhaps better than the text-move which allows the Bishop to enter into play is 41 P—Q 5, P×P; 42 Kt×R P, B—Kt 5; 43 R—B 7, K—B 1; 44 R×R, K×R; 45 Kt—B 5, etc., with a defendable position.

(23) Here is an instance of the danger due to the majority of Pawns on the Queen's side.

(24) Here again very strong play; the Rook is on its way to attack the Pawn on Kt 5 which cannot be defended.

(25) White seizes the only weak chance by exchanging the minor pieces and bringing about a Rook and Pawn ending in which the superiority of one Pawn is not always decisive.

(26) This in connection with the following move constitutes a very risky manoeuvre, but the only means of obtaining a counter attack. Otherwise White would be reduced to complete passivity.

(27) The point of the preceding moves if 52.., P×P than 53 R—Q 4 and White regains the Pawn and through the better position of his Rook obtains a draw.

(28) Owing to the passed Pawn White has good chances of a draw.

(29) If 53.., P—R 6; 54 P×P, R×P; 55 P—Q 6, R—R 2; 56 R—K 5 and White wins one of the united Pawns after which the chances of Black winning would be about equal to those in the actual game.

(30) Far stronger than 58 R×P as Black would then have maintained his crushing Queen's side advantage.

(31) This move forcing the exchange of a further Pawn definitely assures the draw.

(32) As the game is in any case a draw Black might here have tried a very pretty trap: 71.., K—Kt 6 and if 72 R×K R P then 72.., R—K R 5 and wins, White however would probably have taken the right Pawn.

(33) A difficult and instructive end-game.

Game 2.   RUBINSTEIN *v.* ALEKHINE.
Queen's Gambit Declined (in effect).

RUBINSTEIN	ALEKHINE	RUBINSTEIN	ALEKHINE
1 P—Q 4	Kt—K B 3	12 K P×P	P×P
2 P—Q B 4	P—K 3	13 B×P	Kt—Kt 3
3 Kt—Q B 3	P—Q 4	14 B—R 2 (4)	Q Kt—Q 4
4 B—Kt 5	B—K 2	15 B—Kt 1	Kt—Q Kt 5
5 P—K 3	Q Kt—Q 2	16 Q—K 2	B—Q 2
6 Kt—B 3	O—O	17 O—O (5)	B—B 3
7 R—B 1	P—B 3	18 K R—Q 1	K Kt—Q4 (6)
8 Q—B 2	P—K R 3 (1)	19 B—Kt 3	R—B 1
9 B—R 4	P—R 3	20 Kt—K 5	B—K Kt 4 (7)
10 P—R 4 (2)	P—B 4 (3)	21 P—B 4	B—R 5 (8)
11 B—Q 3	P×Q P		*(see diagram)*

Position after 21 P—B 4.

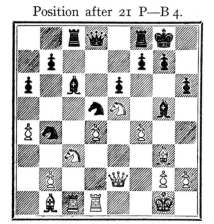

22	Kt × B (9)	R × Kt
23	Kt × Kt	R × R (10)
24	R × R	Kt × Kt
25	Q—K 4	P—K Kt 3
26	B × B	Q × B
27	P—B 5 (11)	Q—Kt 4 (12)
28	R—B 5	Kt P × P
29	Q—B 3	Q—Q 7 (13)
30	Q—Q 3	Q × P
31	P—R 3	K—R 1
32	K—R 2	R—K Kt 1
33	B—B 2	R × P ch
34	K—R 1	Q—B 8 ch
	Resigns (14)	

(1) This move, in combination with 9.., P—R 3 is an innovation of Bogoljubow's first played by him against Euwe in the London tournament, 1922. Rubinstein finds the right reply and remains with a slight advantage.

(2) Burn claims that this leaves a weak spot on Q Kt 4 and points out that Black shortly establishes a Knight on this square. Euwe here played 10 B—Q 3, P × P; 11 B × P, P—Q Kt 4; 12 B—K 2 and Black can at least obtain equality by immediately playing 12.., P—B 4.

(3) Black has here nothing better than to isolate the Queen's Pawn owing to the previous move having prevented the carrying through of Black's original plan—for instance : 10.., P × P; 11 B × P, P—Q Kt 4; 12 B—Q 3, and Black will be unable to advance the Queen's Bishop's Pawn.

(4) Rubinstein plays the first phase of the game in irreproachable style. The permanent threat of mate at K R 7 creates during the subsequent play many difficulties for the defence.

(5) Rightly refusing Black's offer, if 17 B × Kt, B × B; 18 Q—K 4, P—K Kt 3; 19 Q × Kt P, Kt—B 3 ! etc. with advantage.

(6) The best move with a view to obtaining equality. If 19 Q—K 4 Black simply plays 19.., Kt—B 3

(7) The position is now very complicated and most dangerous for Black The move chosen compels White's reply and leads to a crisis.

(8) Black now seeks complications; these however in the present position might conceivably turn to his disadvantage. The following variation has been primarily considered : 21.., B × B P (not 21.., Kt × P; 22 B × Kt, B × B; 23 Kt × B, followed by 24 Q—K 4 winning); 22 Kt × Kt !, Kt × Kt; 23 Kt × B, R × Kt; 24 R × R, P × R; 25 B × B, Kt × B; 26 Q—K 4, Kt—Kt 3; 27 Q × B P, Q—B 1; 28 R—Q B 1, Q × Q !, etc., leading to equality and justifying the previous play.

(9) This leads to nothing—the right continuation (as I pointed out as soon as the game was over) was 22 Kt × Kt ! to which Black would have been forced to reply by 22.., Kt × Kt for if 22.., P × Kt then 23 Q—Kt 4 (or R 5), B × B; 24 Q—B 5, P—K Kt 3; 25 Kt × Kt P and wins. But after 22.., Kt × Kt; 23 Kt × B, P × Kt; 24 Q × R P, B × B; 25 P × B, R—Kt 1 !, etc., to win in spite of being a Pawn up would not have been easy if at all possible !

(10) White had quite possibly not foreseen this reply. Evidently he cannot now play 24 Kt × Kt ? on account of 24.., R × R ch and wins.

(11) A great error of judgment—the game was about equal with a slight balance of advantage (*nuance de supériorite*) for Black due to the commanding position of the Knight if for example 27 P—K Kt 3, Q—Q 1; 28 R—B 5, Q—Kt 3, etc. On the other hand the text move loses off-hand !

(12) White had only considered 27.., Q × Q; 28 B × Q, Kt P × P; 29 B × Kt, P × B; 30 R—B 7 with manifest advantage.

(13) A complete debacle.

(14) If 35 Q—Q 1 Black wins by 35.., Q—B 5 !, etc.

Game 3.		YATES *v.* BOGOLJUBOW.	
		Caro-Kann Defence.	
YATES	BOGOLJUBOW	YATES	BOGOLJUBOW
1 P—K 4	P—Q B 3	18 Q R—B 1	K R—Q 1
2 P—Q 4	P—Q 4	19 P—B 5 (6)	Q Kt—Q 4
3 Kt—Q B 3	P×P	20 Kt—K 5	P—Q Kt 3 ! (7)
4 Kt×P	B—B 4	21 P×P (8)	Q×P
5 Kt—Kt 3	B—Kt 3	22 Kt—B 6 (9)	R—Q 2
6 Kt—B 3	Kt—Q 2	23 Kt×B ch	R×Kt
7 B—Q 3 (1)	K Kt—B 3	24 Kt—K 4	Kt×Kt
8 O—O	P—K 3	25 R×Kt	R—Q 2
9 R—K 1	B—K 2 (2)	26 K R—Q B 4	Q R—Q 1
10 Q—K 2 (3)	B×B	27 P—K R 3	Q—Kt 1 (10)
11 Q×B	O—O	28 B—K 1 (11)	Kt—B 5
12 B—Kt 5	P—K R 3	29 Q—K B 3 (12)	Kt—Q 6
13 B—Q 2	P—B 4 (4)	30 Q—K 2	Kt×R
14 P×P	B×P	31 R×Kt	Q—B 5
15 P—Kt 4 !	B—K 2	32 R—B 4	R—Q 5
16 P—B 4 (5)	Kt—Kt 3	33 P—Kt 3	Q—B 4
17 Q—Kt 3	Q—B 2	34 R—B 5	Q—Kt 8
		Resigns	

(1) Generally P—K R 4 is played first in order to force a weakening on Black's King's side and consequently Castling on this side is then impossible. The line of play adopted by White creates but little difficulty for Black. Burn suggests B—Q B 4.

(2) He could also play 9.., B—Q 3 for 10 Kt—B 5, B×Kt; 11 B×B, Castles; 12 B—Q 3, Q—B 2, etc., was not to be feared.

(3) In order to play 11 Kt—B 5 should Black Castle.

(4) Black has already a fairly equal game, but the text is a grave error of judgment, giving to White a Pawn superiority on the Queen's side without reason or compensation. 13.., Q—Kt 3 followed by 14.., K R—Q 1 was clearly indicated.

(5) White's advantage is here quite evident.

(6) The first mistake which gives Black an important post for his Knight at Q 4. By simply playing 19 P—Q R 4 and 20 P—R 5 White strengthens the pressure on the Queen's side without risk, and it is difficult to see how Black can proceed.

(7) A master stroke which nullifies almost completely White's advantage for if 21 P—B 6, P—Q Kt 4 followed by 22.., B—Q 3 and the advanced Pawn becomes a source of weakness.

(8) Whilst in this variation the extra Pawn on the Queen's side will not make itself felt until very much later, if at all.

(9) The exchanges which result are certainly not to the disadvantage of Black, but White has evidently lost the thread of the game.

(10) A strong move which takes advantage of the uncomfortable position of the White Bishop, for it threatens 28.., Kt—Kt 3. Black's position is now superior.

(11) In any case White should have prevented entry of the Knight at B 5. Less dangerous surely would have been 28 B—K 3, Kt×B; 29 P×Kt, R—Q 6; 30 Q×R, etc., with a game still defensible.

(12) A second error which loses the Exchange and the game. After 29 Q—K 3, P—K 4, etc., and Black has much the best of it.

ROUND II

Game 4.   ALEKHINE *v.* TARRASCH.

Queen's Gambit Declined.

	ALEKHINE	TARRASCH		ALEKHINE	TARRASCH
1	P—Q 4	P—Q 4	24	Q Kt×R P	Kt—K 5
2	P—Q B 4	P—Q B 3	25	Kt—B 6 (15)	P—Kt 4
3	Kt—K B 3	Kt—B 3	26	B—K 5	Kt×B
4	Kt—B 3	P×P (1)	27	Q Kt×Kt	P—B 3 (16)
5	P—K 3 (2)	P—Q Kt 4	28	Q×Kt	P×Kt
6	P—Q R 4	P—Kt 5 (3)	29	P—Q 6	B—Kt 2
7	Kt—R 2 (4)	P—K 3	30	Q—Q 5 ch	K—R 1
8	B×P	B—K 2 (5)	31	Q×B P	Resigns
9	O—O	O—O			
10	Q—K 2	B—Kt 2			
11	R—Q 1	Q Kt—Q 2			
12	P—K 4 (6)	P—Q R 4 (7)			
13	B—K Kt 5	R—K 1			
14	Kt—B 1 (8)	Q—Kt 3			
15	Kt—Kt 3 (9)	P—R 3 (10)			
16	B—K 3	B—R 3 (11)			
17	K Kt—Q 2 (12)	B×B			
18	Kt×B	Q—B 2			
19	Q—B 3	P—B 4 (13)			
20	B—B 4	Q—Kt 2			
21	P—Q 5	P×P			
22	P×P	Q—R 3			

Position after 22.., Q—R 3.

(See diagram).

23 Q R—B 1 (14)   B—B 1

(1) This variation which exacts a fairly deep study before being ventured was tried by me on two occasions in the London tournament, 1922 (against Bogoljubow and Rubinstein). I was therefore surprised to find Dr. Tarrasch using my own weapons against me !

(2) I consider this move to be stronger than 5 P—Q R 4 as played in the above-mentioned two games.

(3) This move, which I used in several of my games against the eminent problemist, Valentin Marin, during my recent stay in Spain, constitutes one of the salient points of my system. If White answers by 7 Kt—Q Kt 1 Black can retain the Pawn temporarily by 7.., B—R 3 !; 8 Kt—K 5, Q—Q 4. Burn considers that having captured the Pawn, Black's best chance is to try to retain it by 6.., Q—Kt 3, etc.

(4) This move wins back the Pawn immediately and the sole inconvenience to White's game will consist of the unfavourable situation of the Knight. Against this must be set off Black's weakened Queen's side.

(5) Black neglects both here and with the play that follows to advance the Bishop's Pawn. This would have given counter attacking chances. If this variation is at all playable it is only possible in combination with 8..., B—Kt 2 followed by 9.., P—B 4, etc.

(6) Having secured the centre squares and prevented the advance of the Bishop's Pawn, White now commands the Board.

(7) Forced sooner or later.

(8) By this means the last drawback is eliminated and the hitherto badly placed Knight comes back into the fray.

(9) One may notice this position and manoeuvre of the Knights in analogous positions in many of my games, notably those against Maroczy and Rubinstein at the Hague tournament in 1921.

(10) Trying to relieve the pressure; an attempt which only accentuates his disadvantage.

(11) If 16.., Kt×P; 17 P—Q 5! followed by 18 P×K P, winning easily.

(12) Not 17 P—Q 5, B×B; 18 Q×B, B P×P; 19 P×P, P×P; 20 R×P, Q—K 3, etc., and Black's defence is sufficient.

(13) Too late! This move now allows White to get a strong passed Pawn.

(14) Decisive; the Queen's Rook's Pawn could not be captured by either the Queen's Knight on account of 23.., B—Q 1 or by the King's Knight on account of 23.., P—B 5, now, however, it must fall and the game goes with it.

(15) Possibly the most difficult move in the game. White here abandons the passed Rook's Pawn in order to capture one of Black's, as follows: 25.., Q×P; 26 B×P, P×B; 27 Q—Kt 4 ch, followed by 28 Q×Q Kt. Black's attempt to obviate this line of play ends in an immediate loss.

(16) Evidently the only move.

Game 5.   BOGOLJUBOW *v.* RUBINSTEIN.

Four Knights' Game (Double Ruy Lopez).

	BOGOLJUBOW	RUBINSTEIN		BOGOLJUBOW	RUBINSTEIN
1	P—K 4	P—K 4	29	P—R 4	B—K 1 (10)
2	Kt—K B 3	Kt—Q B 3	30	P—Q R 5	P—Kt 4 (11)
3	Kt—B 3	Kt—B 3	31	B×P (12)	R—Kt 1
4	B—Kt 5	B—Kt 5 (1)	32	P—B 4	K—K 2 (13)
5	O—O	O—O	33	K R—Kt 3	B—R 4
6	P—Q 3	P—Q 3	34	R—K B 1 (14)	R×R P
7	B—Kt 5	B×Kt	35	K—Kt 3	R—B 5
8	P×B	Q—K 2 (2)	36	Q R—Q Kt 1	R—Kt 2 (15)
9	R—K 1	Kt—Q 1	37	R—K R 1	B—Kt 3 (16)
10	P—Q 4	B—Kt 5 (3)	38	R—Q 3 (17)	R—Kt 1
11	P—K R 3	B—R 4	39	Q R—Q 1	Q R—K B 1
12	P—Kt 4	B—Kt 3	40	R—Kt 3 (18)	R×P ch
13	B—Q 3	Kt—K 3	41	R×R	R×R ch
14	B—Q B 1	Kt—Q 2	42	K×R	B—R 4 ch
15	R—Kt 1	P—Kt 3	43	K—Kt 3	B×R
16	K—Kt 2!	P—Q B 4 (4)	44	B—B 6	K×P
17	P—Q 5	Kt—B 5 ch	45	B—Q 5 ch	K—K 2
18	B×Kt	P×B	46	P—B 3	B—R 4 (19)
19	Q—Q 2	Q—B 3 (5)	47	B—B 6	B—B 2
20	P—Kt 5 (6)	Q—K 2	48	B—Kt 5	B—K 3
21	Q×P	P—B 3	49	K—R 4	K—Q 1
22	Q—Kt 4	R—B 2 (7)	50	K—Kt 3	K—B 2
23	P—K R 4	Kt—K 4	51	K—B 3	K—Kt 2
24	Kt×Kt	B P×Kt	52	K—B 3	K—B 2
25	P—B 3	R—B 5 (8)	53	K—B 3	B—Q 2
	(*See diagram*).		54	K—Kt 3	B—B 3 (20)
26	Q—K 6 ch	Q×Q	55	K—B 3	P—K R 3
27	P×Q (9)	B—R 4	56	P×P	P×P
28	R—K 3	K—B 1	57	K—Kt 3	P—R 4

58	K—B 3	P—R 5	77 K—Q 2	K—R 5
59	K—Kt 4	B×P	78 K—B 2	K—R 6
60	K×P	B—Q 6	Resigns	
61	K—Kt 4	P—Q 4	Position after 25 P—B 3.	
62	K—B 3	B×P		
63	B×B	P×B		
64	K—K 4	K—Q 3		
65	K—B 5	P—R 3		
66	K—K 4	K—K 3		
67	K—K 3	K—B 4		
68	K—B 3	P—K 5 ch		
69	K—K 3	K—K 4		
70	K—K 2	K—B 5		
71	K—B 2	P—K 6 ch		
72	K—K 1	K—K 4		
73	K—Q 1	K—Q 4		
74	K—K 1	K—B 3		
75	K—K 2	K—Kt 4		
76	K×P	K×P		

(1) It is interesting to note that Rubinstein here refrains from playing his own, and in my opinion, very strong defence 4.., Kt—Q 5. Probably on account of the bad result he had with it against his present opponent in their match in Sweden in 1920.

(2) This defence was also played with success by Rubinstein some fifteen years previously. Since then he has dropped it. Is it his intention to revive it ?

(3) The usual continuation is 10.., Kt—K 3 ; 11 B—Q B 1 (Teichmann), P—B 3. The manoeuvre with the Bishop induces White to attack with his King's side Pawns which, whilst apparently hopeful, is seen in the sequel to produce some weak spots.

(4) This move at first sight seems inferior as it robs the Queen's Knight of his best square and allows White to block the centre without adding to his weaknesses. In reality it is the beginning of a long combination, in the course of which Black sacrifices a Pawn in order to weaken White's hold on the Black squares. As the sequel proves, Black has established a sound position which only bad tactics can spoil.

(5) Inviting White's reply in order to secure the open King's Bishop's file.

(6) No better would have been 20 P—K R 4 for 20.., P—K R 4 ; 21 P—Kt 5, Q—K 2 ; 22 Q×P, P—B 3, etc., and White has not even the square, Kt 4 for his Queen.

(7) A shrewd move to enable him to play 23.., Kt—K 4 without being open to a forced exchange of Queens.

(8) A grave mistake, the more incomprehensible as Black had sought to prevent the exchange two moves previously. The correct line was 25.., Q—B 1 followed by 26.., R—B 5, 27.., B—R 4, etc., then Q R—K B 2 *via* K 1 and K 2, etc.

(9) By this exchange White has at last got a game. Black's Queen's Pawn is weak, and in certain variations the advance of White's P—K 7 may become very dangerous.

(10) Rubinstein is evidently demoralised by having ruined his position, and allows himself to be drawn into an unsound combination. The logical continuation was 29.., K—K 2 ; 30 P—R 5, R—Q Kt 1, etc.

(11) Here again 30.., R—Kt 1 is necessary. The text-move should have led to a loss.

(12) A sacrifice, but in reality a Greek gift. It is really astonishing that Rubinstein had not contemplated the consequences which are evident enough.

(13) A sad necessity, for after 32.., P—Q R 3 ; 33 K R—Kt 3, P×B ; 34 P×P, etc. Black would have no defence against the passed Pawns. As it is Black is not only two Pawns down but has the inferior position.

(14) It is now White's turn to blunder. Still this one is not decisive. The simple move 34 K—Kt 3 wins quickly, *e.g.*, 34.., Q R—K B I ; 35 R—K B I, R×K P ; 36 P×R, R×R ; 37 B—B 6, K×P ; 38 R—Kt 7 and mate follows. Other variations are similar.

(15) If 36.., Q R—K B I ; 37 B—B 6 and has a similar win to that in the last note.

(16) Forced, for after 37.., P—Kt 3 the Bishop is permanently shut out.

(17) An unexpected attack on the Queen's Pawn which should have been decisive.

(18) This shows the fatal effect of one lapse in a winning position. Instead of the text, 40 R—Q Kt I, R—Q Kt I ; 41 Q R—Kt 3 followed by 42 B—B 6 forces Black's resignation in a few moves. Bogoljubow puts as it were, the whole game *en prise*.

(19) Black is now a Pawn to the good, and moreover, his position is superior. Rubinstein's method of winning is interesting, although the position presents no difficulties. The text-move intends to force exchange of Bishops.

(20) White dare not exchange the Bishops as his Rook's Pawn would fall.

Game 6.   YATES *v.* THOMAS.

Ruy Lopez (Morphy Defence).

	YATES	THOMAS		YATES	THOMAS
1	P—K 4	P—K 4	20	Q R—K I	P—B 4
2	Kt—K B 3	Kt—Q B 3	21	Q—K 3	R—R 2
3	B—Kt 5	P—Q R 3	22	P—Kt 4	Kt×P
4	B—R 4	Kt—B 3	23	P×Kt	B×B
5	O—O	Kt×P	24	R—K 2	R—B 2
6	P—Q 4	P—Q Kt 4	25	Q—Q 3	Kt—Kt 4
7	B—Kt 3	P—Q 4	26	R×R ch	K×R
8	P×P	B—K 3	27	Q—K 3	R—K 2
9	P—B 3	B—K 2	28	Q×R ch	Q×Q
10	Q Kt—Q 2	O—O	29	R×Q	K×R
11	B—B 2 (1)	P—B 4	30	Kt×P	B×P
12	P×P *e.p.*	Kt×P (B 3)	31	Kt×P	Kt—B 6 ch
13	Kt—Kt 5 (2)	B—K Kt 5 (3)	32	K—R I	Kt—K 8
14	P—B 3	B—B I	33	B—Kt I	B—R 6
15	Kt—Kt 3 (4)	P—R 3	34	K—Kt I (6)	Kt—B 6 ch
16	Q—Q 3 (5)	P×Kt	35	K—R I	K—Q 3
17	B×P	Kt—K 4	36	Kt—Kt 4	B—B 7
18	Q—Q 4	Kt—B 2	37	Kt—Q 3	B—K 6
19	B—R 4	Q—Q 3		Resigns (7)	

(1) A good variant proposed by Dr. Olland is 11 R—K 1, Kt—B 4 ; 12 Kt—B 1, etc.

(2) A premature attacking move which soon creates many difficulties for White. The usual move is 13 Kt—Kt 3 and if 13.., B—K Kt 5 ; 14 Q—Q 3, Kt—K 5 ; 15 Q Kt—Q 4 with equal chances.

(3) In order to cut off the best line of retreat for White's Knight.

(4) Having already in view the possibility of leaving the Knight *en prise* in reply to Black's next move. Otherwise the only move was 15 Q—K 1 and if 15.., Q—Q 3 ; 16 P—K B 4, etc., at least without material loss.

(5) An astonishing move which surrenders a piece for nothing. Certainly White's position was not enviable after 16 Kt—R 3, B × Kt ; 17 P × B, Q—Q 3 ; 18 K—Kt 2, but after the text move it is hopeless. The rest needs little comment.

(6) Black threatened 34.., B—B 7 followed by 35.., B—Kt 7 mate.

(7) For Black wins another piece by 38.., Kt—R 5 ; 39 Kt—K 1, B—B 7, etc.

ROUND III

Game 7.　　　　THOMAS *v.* ALEKHINE.

Ruy Lopez (Morphy Defence).

	THOMAS	ALEKHINE
1	P—K 4	P—K 4
2	Kt—K B 3	Kt—Q B 3
3	B—Kt 5	P—Q R 3
4	B—R 4	Kt—B 3
5	Kt—B 3 (1)	B—K 2
6	O—O	P—Q Kt 4
7	B—Kt 3	P—Q 3
8	P—Q R 4	P—Kt 5 (2)
9	Kt—Q 5	Kt—Q R 4
10	Kt × B (3)	Q × Kt
11	P—Q 4 (4)	Kt × B
12	P × Kt	B—Kt 5 (5)
13	B—Kt 5	O—O (6)
14	P—Q 5 (7)	P—R 3
15	B × Kt	Q × B
16	R—B 1	Q—B 5 (8)
17	Q—Q 3	P—K B 4
18	Kt—Q 2	P × P
19	Kt × P	R—B 2 (9)
20	R—B 4	B—B 4
21	R × Kt P	P—Q R 4
22	R—B 4	R—Kt 1 (10)
23	P—B 3	Q—Kt 4 (11)
24	Q—B 3	Q—Kt 3
25	P—Q Kt 4 (12)	B × Kt
26	R × B	P × P
27	R × Kt P	R × R
28	Q × R	Q—Q 6 (13)
29	P—R 5 (14)	Q—K 6 ch
30	K—R 1	P—K 5 (15)

Position after 30 K—R 1.

	THOMAS	ALEKHINE
31	Q—B 3	Q—K 7
32	R—K 1 (16)	Q—Kt 4 (17)
33	Q—B 6 (18)	Q × R P
34	Q—K 8 ch	R—B 1
35	Q × P	Q—Q 7
36	P—Q Kt 3	R—B 5
37	Q—K 6 ch	K—R 2
38	P—R 3	Q—Q 6
39	R—K 3 (18a)	Q—Kt 8 ch
40	K—R 2	Q—B 7 (19)
41	K—Kt 3 (20)	R—B 3
42	Q—K 4 ch (21)	R—Kt 3 ch
43	K—R 4	Q × K Kt P
44	P—B 4	Q × Q (22)

45	R×Q	R—Kt 8	
46	R—B 4	K—Kt 3	
47	R×P	K—B 4 (23)	
48	R—Q 7	K×P	
49	R×Q P	R—Kt 6 (24)	
50	R—Q 8	P—Kt 4 ch	
51	K—R 5	R×P ch	
52	K—Kt 6	K—K 4	
53	P—Q 6	K—K 3	
54	P—Kt 4	P—Kt 5	
55	P—Q 7 (25)	P—Kt 6	
56	R—K Kt 8	K×P	
57	K—B 5	P—R 4	
58	K—B 4	P—R 5 (26)	
59	P—Kt 5	K—B 2	
60	R—Kt 6	R—R 7	
61	K—B 3	K—Kt 2 (27)	
62	P—Kt 6	K—R 3	
63	P—Kt 7 dis ch	K×P	
64	R—Kt 7 ch	K—B 3	

65	R—Kt 6 ch	K—Q 4	
66	R—Kt 8	K—K 3 (28)	
67	R—Kt 5	K—B 2	
68	R—Kt 4	K—B 3	
69	R—Kt 8	K—B 4	
70	R—B 8 ch	K—Kt 4	
71	R—Kt 8 ch	K—B 3 (29)	
72	R—Kt 4	K—B 4	
73	R—Kt 8	K—K 4	
74	R—K 8 ch	K—Q 5 (30)	
75	R—K Kt 8	K—Q 6	
76	R—Q 8 ch	K—B 6	
77	R—K Kt 8	K—Q 7	
78	R—Q R 8	R—B 7 ch	
79	K—Kt 4	P—Kt 7	
80	R—R 1	K—K 6	
81	K—R 3	R—K 7	
82	K—K Kt 1	K—B 6	
83	K—R 2	P—R 6	

Resigns (31)

(1) I tried this line of attack, recommended by Dr. Tarrasch, in the recent tournament at Pištyan against Bogoljubow. The result was, however, not satisfactory and I was therefore inclined to believe that the variation was unsound. The continuation adopted by Sir George Thomas (recommended by Svenonius) proved that I was mistaken.

(2) Perhaps a little better is 8.., Q R—Kt 1, although White still obtains a slight advantage by playing 9 P×P, P×P; 10 P—R 3, O—O; 11 P—Q 3, etc.

(3) My game with Bogoljubow (Pistyan, 1922) was continued as follows: 10 Kt×Kt ch, B×Kt; 11 B—Q 5, P—B 3; 12 B—R 2, P—B 4! with advantage to Black.

(4) A simple and powerful move. White does not fear the exchange of the Bishop for the Knight as the open file is sufficient compensation.

(5) An alternative was 12.., B—Kt 2; 13 B—Kt 5, B×P; 14 R—K 1 B×Kt; 15 Q×B, O—O; 16 Q R—B 1, with the threat 17 P×P, P×P; 18 R—B 6 and much the superior position.

(6) Naturally not 13.., B×Kt; 14 Q×B, P×P, on account of 15 P—K 5, etc.

(7) With this move White pins down the weak points in his adversary's game and forces Black to seek at all costs some compensation on the King's wing. The game soon gets very lively.

(8) In making this move Black had decided to give up the Queen's Knight's Pawn so as to gain time to open the King's Bishop's file. The passive defence by 16.., Q R—B 1 would have led in the long run to certain defeat.

(9) To 19.., Q—B 2 White would likewise have replied 20 R—B 4 with the double threat of R×Kt P and also Kt×P.

(10) 22.., R—Q B 1 was insufficient on account of 23 Kt×P, P—K 5; 24 Kt×R, etc. [This note does not seem correct, because if 23 Kt×P then B×Q appears to be better than P—K 5 (Editor).]

(11) This manoeuvre of the Queen is necessary so as to increase the power of Black's other pieces. White does not obtain any advantage by 24 Kt×Q, B×Q; 25 Kt×R, B×Q R; 26 Kt×P ch, P×Kt; 27 P×B, R×P, etc.

(12) The capture of the Bishop's Pawn was far from being decisive for example : 25 R×P, R×P! ; 26 Q×R, R×R, and White cannot continue 27 Q—Kt 8 ch followed by 28 Q×P on account of 28.., B×Kt winning. So White creates instead winning chances through the possession of a passed Pawn.

(13) By this strong move Black succeeds in maintaining equality. Owing to the weak position of White's Queen's Pawn and the unfavourable position of the King due to the advance of the King's Bishop's Pawn Black has now sufficient compensation for the sacrificed Pawn.

(14) Energetically played ! White does not fear the loss of the Queen's Pawn as in that case his passed Pawn would become formidable. Insufficient would have been 29 Q—K 4 on account of 29.., Q—Q 7 followed by 30.., R—B 5, etc.

(15) The position has now become very interesting. White cannot obtain anything by 31 Q—K 1, Q—Q 6 ; 32 Q—Q 1, Q—Kt 4 or by 31 R—K 1, R×P! ! ; 32 P×R, Q×P ch, and draws by perpetual check.

(16) There is nothing better.

(17) Black plays here too subtly, not wishing to exchange Pawns and thus open the King's file—a futile precaution. The simple variation, 32.., P×P! ; 33 P×P, Q—Kt 4, etc., leaves no advantage to White—taking into consideration the general weakness of his Pawn position.

(18) Now White, by sacrificing his passed Pawn for Black's King's Pawn still maintains his advantage.

(18a) *The Field* suggests that 39 Q—K 3 is superior, as follows :　39.., Q×Q ; 40 R×Q R—Q 5 ; 41 R—B 3 with good winning chances.

(19) White has succeeded in defending his Pawn, but his pieces are fixed, and it is not apparent how the material advantage could be turned to account ; an attempt might be made as follows : 41 Q—K 7, R—Q 5 ; 42 P—B 4 (or 42 R—K 4, R×P ; 43 R—K Kt 4, R—K Kt 4 ; 44 R×R, P×R ; 45 Q×Kt P, Q×P, etc.) ; 42.., R×B P ; 43 R—Kt 3, Q—Kt 7 ; 44 Q×B P, Q—K 4 and White cannot hope to win. The 41st move made by White is a miscalculation which loses his Pawn and can only lead him henceforth to look for a draw,

(20) Overlooking the check in reply to his own.

(21) Simpler, so as to secure the draw, would have been 42 R—K 2 !, Q×P ; 43 Q—K 4 ch, K—Kt 1, etc. In spite of the text-move the game can, however, still be saved.

(22) By means of this Exchange Black obtains a slightly better Rook ending.

(23) Threatening to win the Queen's Pawn by 48.., K—K 5, which would lead to a decisive advantage.

(24) The point of the previous manoeuvres—creating two united passed Pawns.

(25) In this difficult position White misses the correct continuation. His last chance of securing a draw was with the following play : 55 P—Kt 5 ! and if 55.., P—Kt 6 ; 56 K—R 7 !!, etc. After the text-move the game is irretrievably lost.

(26) The win is now easy ; it consists first in winning the adverse Pawn with the King. This is easily accomplished through White exhausting his moves. and then the remainder is merely a matter of routine.

(27) The first phase is now over ; the Rook must move, still holding on to the Knight's file, and the Black King now approaches the adverse passed Pawn. If in this position it was Black's turn to move the winning procedure would be as follows : 61..,K—B 2 ; 62 R—B 6 ch, K—Q 1 ! ; 63 R—K Kt 6, K—Q 2 ; 64 R—Kt 7 ch, K—B 1 ; 65 P—Kt 6, K—Kt 1, etc.

(28) 66.., K—Q 5 would have shortened the game by about ten moves.

(29) Black could also play here 71.., K—R 3 ; 72 K—B 4, P—Kt 7 ; 73 K—B 5, P—R 6 ; 74 K—B 6, K—R 2 ; 75 R—Kt 7 ch, K—R 1 and White cannot draw by perpetual.

(30) Reproducing a position of Kling's.

(31) If 84 K×P, R—K 1 ; 85 K—R 4, R—R 1 ch ; 86 K—Kt 5, R—R 8 winning.

Game 8.   TARRASCH *v.* BOGOLJUBOW.

Giuoco Piano.

TARRASCH	BOGOLJUBOW	TARRASCH	BOGOLJUBOW
1 P—K 4	P—K 4	38 R—R 3	R—Q 2
2 Kt—K B 3	Kt—Q B 3	39 K R—Q R 1	P—R 4 (13)
3 B—B 4	B—B 4	Position after 39 K R—Q R 1.	
4 P—Q 3	P—Q 3		
5 Kt—B 3	Kt—B 3		
6 B—K 3	B—Kt 3		
7 Q—Q 2 (1)	B—Kt 5		
8 O—O—O (2)	B—Q R 4		
9 Q—K 2 (3)	B×Q Kt		
10 P×B	P—Q 4		
11 B—Kt 3	Q—Q 3		
12 P—K R 3	B×Kt (4)		
13 Q×B	P—Q 5		
14 P×P	Kt×Q P		
15 B×Kt	Q×B	40 R×P	R×R
16 Q—K 3 (5)	Q—B 6	41 R×R	R—B 2
17 Q—K 1	Q—R 8 ch	42 P—Kt 3	P—R 5
18 K—Q 2	Q—Q 5	43 P×P (14)	Kt—R 4
19 Q—K 3	Q—Q 3	44 K—B 3	K—K 2
20 K R—B 1	O—O	45 B—Q 5	Kt—B 5
21 P—K B 4	Q R—Q 1	46 K—Kt 4	Kt—Kt 7
22 P—B 5 (6)	P—Q Kt 4	47 B—Kt 3 (15)	P—B 5
23 K—K 2	P—Q R 4	48 P×P	Kt—K 6 ch
24 P—Q R 4 (7)	P×P	49 K—B 3	Kt×P (B 5)
25 B×P	Q—Kt 5	50 B×Kt (16)	R×B
26 R—Q R 1	R—Q 5	51 R×P ch	K—B 3
27 K—B 3	Q—B 6	52 R—K 8	R×B P
28 K R—K 1 (8)	K R—Q 1	53 K—Kt 4	R—Kt 7 ch
29 K R—Q B 1 (9)	P—R 3	54 K—B 4	R—B 7 ch
30 K—B 2	R—Kt 5	55 K—Kt 3	R—K 7
31 B—Kt 3	P—B 4 (10)	56 P—R 5	R—K 8
32 Q—K 1	Q—Q 5 ch	57 K—B 2	R—K R 8
33 Q—K 3	Q—B 6	Drawn	
34 Q—K 1	Q—Q 5 ch		
35 Q—K 3	R—R 1 (11)		
36 Q×Q	R×Q		
37 K—K 3 (12)	K—B 1		

(1) This variation was sometimes played by Tchigorin, but without success. Black has no difficulty in developing.

(2) Relatively better was 8 Kt—K Kt 5, B—K R 4 ; 9 P—B 3, etc., as played amongst others by Tartakower and Rubinstein at Göteberg, 1920. After the text-move the White pieces remain cramped and 8 O—O—O results in a weakening of the King's position.

(3) The best move in view of the threatened 9.., Kt—Q 5

(4) Black has a much superior game, but the series of Exchanges initiated by this move lessen his chance of attack. On the one hand the simplification

is not to his advantage and on the other White's Bishop proves much more powerful than the opposing Knight. The simple move, 12.., B—R 4, keeping up the pressure, would have maintained the superiority.

(5) From here to move 35 White, with commendable perseverance, seeks to exchange Queens, showing clearly by repetition of moves that he would be satisfied with a draw. Black, in avoiding the exchange at any cost drifts, as often happens, into a lost position.

(6) Opening the Bishop's file was not to be recommended seeing the precarious position of the White King which is now sheltered.

(7) The only thing to do, but quite good enough. The passed Pawn that Black now obtains is held by the Bishop and will in the end be actually a weakness. If Black blocks the Queen's side by 24.., P—Kt 5 White will have time for a counter demonstration on the King's side by 25 P—Kt 4, etc.

(8) The object of this move is not evident, better was at once 28 K R—B 1

(9) The easiest way of meeting the threatened 29.., R × Q P, etc

(10) If Black still was playing for a win he should have tried 31.., Kt—Q 2 followed by 32.., Kt—B 4, etc. The text-move abandons the square Q 5 to the White Bishop, and puts Black in the inferior position for the end-game, and in a few moves he should have been content with a draw.

(11) Black should have repeated the moves, for his obstinate persistence in playing for a win without justification should have cost the game.

(12) On account of the threat 37.., P—B 5 and 38.., Kt × P ch.

(13) An act of despair but quite comprehensible for the defence of the Pawn by 39.., Q R—R 2 would have led after 40 K—B 3, 41 P—Kt 4, 42 R—R 4 and 43 B—B 4 to a position where Black could only move his King, whilst White quietly prepares the advance of King's side Pawns and forces the fatal dislodgment of the Knight.

(14) This also should win, but why not simply 43 P—Kt 4. It is evident Black could never play Kt—R 2 and Kt 4 safely because of R—R 8 ch, followed by R—R 8 winning.

(15) A singular aberration. Instead of further strengthening the position of his Bishop by 47 P—B 4 which would have left Black without resource, *viz.*, 47.., Kt—B 5; 48 R—R 3, K—B 3; 49 P—R 5, followed by 50 R—R 6 ch and 51 P—R 6, etc., White finds the only move which allows Black to try for a draw. In this game Bogoljubow was favoured by fortune.

(16) The final blunder. 50 R—Q 5 still offered winning chances. As played the game is definitely drawn despite the extra Pawns. The latter part of the game is not in Tarrasch's form of other days.

Game 9.   Rubinstein *v.* Yates.
              King's Knight's Gambit.

Rubinstein	Yates	Rubinstein	Yates
1 P—K 4	P—K 4	12 B—Q 2 (5)	Kt—B 3
2 P—K B 4	P × P	13 O—O—O	O—O—O
3 Kt—K B 3	Kt—K B 3 (1)	14 P—K R 4	P—B 3
4 Kt—B 3	P—Q 4	15 P—B 4 (6)	Q × Kt P (7)
5 P × P	Kt × P	16 P × P	P × P
6 Kt × Kt	Q × Kt	17 P—Q 5	Kt—Kt 5 (8)
7 P—Q 4	B—K 2 (2)	18 Q × B	Kt—Q 6 ch
8 B—Q 3	P—K Kt 4	19 K—B 2	Q × Kt
9 Q—K 2	B—B 4	20 Q—K 6 ch	K—Kt 1
10 B × B	Q × B	21 R—R 3	Q × R ch (9)
11 P—K Kt 4 (3)	Q—Q 2 (4)	(*see diagram*)	

Position after 21 R—R 3.

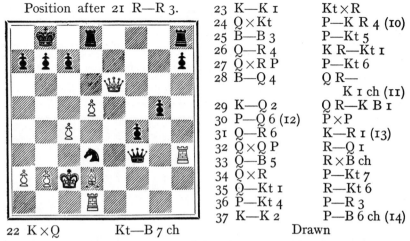

	23 K—K 1	Kt × R
	24 Q × Kt	P—K R 4 (10)
	25 B—B 3	P—Kt 5
	26 Q—R 4	K R—Kt 1
	27 Q × R P	P—Kt 6
	28 B—Q 4	Q R—
		K 1 ch (11)
	29 K—Q 2	Q R—K B 1
	30 P—Q 6 (12)	P × P
	31 Q—R 6	K—R 1 (13)
	32 Q × Q P	R—Q 1
	33 Q—B 5	R × B ch
	34 Q × R	P—Kt 7
	35 Q—Kt 1	R—Kt 6
	36 P—Kt 4	P—R 3
	37 K—K 2	P—B 6 ch (14)

22 K × Q   Kt—B 7 ch   Drawn

(1) 3.., P—K Kt 4 is more usual, but the text move is quite good and was made to avoid regular lines.

(2 This very strong move, which permits defence of the gambit Pawn, throws some doubt upon the correctness of the variation adopted by White.

(3) Up to this move, very ingenious but not sufficient as the present game shows, both players have repeated the moves of the game Rubinstein *v*. Kostich, Hague, 1921.

(4) Kostich here played 11.., Q—K 3 and obtained after 12 Q × Q, P × Q; 13 P—K R 4. P × P; 14 P—Kt 5, a game by no means satisfactory. After the text move Black gets an evident advantage.

(5) No better was 12 Kt × P, Kt—B 3; 13 B × P, Kt × P; 14 Q—K 4, O—O—O; 15 O—O—O, Q × P; 16 R × Kt, B × Kt; 17 Q—K 5, B × B ch; 18 R × B, Q—Kt 7, etc., with a clear advantage for Black.

(6) Rubinstein makes praiseworthy efforts to bring about complications, but he should not succeed.

(7) An involved and useless combination which eventually allows White to save the game. The simple move 15.., Q R—K 1 would preserve the advantage without difficulty, *e.g.*, 16 P × P, P × P; 17 P—Q 5, Kt—Q 1; 18 Kt—K 5, B—Q 3, etc.

(8) If 17.., Kt—Kt 1; 18 Q R—Kt 1, Q—Q 2; 19 B—B 3, etc.

(9) The sacrifice of the Queen was forced. Black was rightly afraid of the variation 21.., Kt—B 4; 22 R × Q, Kt × Q; 23 P × Kt, K R—K 1; 24 R—K 1, R—Q 3; 25 R—Q 3 which would lead to a lost game for him.

(10) These three passed Pawns now constitute a formidable force and all the mastery of a Rubinstein is necessary to stop them in time.

(11) Yates plays this end-game very correctly. The check is just in time, for 29 K—B 1 would now lead to a loss on account of 29.., P—B 6, etc.

(12) White could no longer hope for a win by continuing 30 Q—B 3, P—Kt 7; 31 B—Kt 1, R—Kt 6; 32 Q—B 2, P—Kt 3; 33 P—R 4, R—Kt 3 with the threat 34.., P—B 6, etc. The variation in the text which forces the draw is therefore the simplest and best method of liquidating the adventurous enterprise which the King's Gambit always entails for White.

(13) The correct reply. Black again intends to sacrifice the exchange in order to fix the opposing pieces to the passed Pawns.

(14) This move forces the sequel, 38 K—B 2, R—R 6; 39 Q—Q 1, R—R 8; 40 Q—Q 8 ch and draw by perpetual check. A much admired game, played on both sides with much spirit. Diamond cut diamond throughout.

ROUND IV

Game 10.   ALEKHINE *v.* YATES.

Queen's Gambit Declined.

	ALEKHINE	YATES
1	P—Q 4	Kt—K B 3
2	Kt—K B 3	P—Q 4
3	P—B 4	P—K 3
4	B—Kt 5	B—K 2 (1)
5	P—K 3	O—O
6	Q Kt—Q 2 (2)	P—Q Kt 3
7	B—Q 3	B—Kt 2
8	Q—B 2	Q Kt—Q 2
9	O—O	P—B 4
10	Q R—Q 1	P—K R 3
11	B—R 4	P × Q P (3)
12	K P × P	P × P
13	B × P	R—B 1
14	Q—Q 3	Kt—Q 4
15	B—K Kt 3	Q Kt—B 3
16	P—Q R 3 (4)	Kt—R 4
17	Q—K 4	Kt × B (5)
18	R P × Kt	R—B 2
19	B—Q 3	Kt—B 3
20	Q—K 2	Q—Q 4
21	Kt—B 4	Q—K R 4 (6)
22	Q Kt—K 5	K R—B 1
23	K R—K 1	B—Q 3
24	B—Kt 1 (7)	Kt—Kt 5
25	Kt—R 4 (8)	B × Kt
26	P × B	P—K Kt 4
27	P—B 3 (9)	P × Kt
28	P × Kt	Q—Kt 4
29	P × P	Q × R P
30	Q—Q 3	Q—Kt 4 (10)
31	R—K B 1	B—Q 4 (11)
32	Q—R 7 ch	K—B 1 (12)

(See diagram).

Position after 32.., K—B 1.

	ALEKHINE	YATES
33	R × B	P × R
34	B—Kt 6	K—K 1
35	R × P (13)	R—B 8 ch
36	K—B 2 (14)	Q—R 5 ch
37	K—K 3	Q—K 8 ch
38	K—B 3	K R—B 6 ch
39	P × R	R × P ch
40	B—Q 3	Q—B 8 ch
41	K—K 3 (15)	R × B ch (16)
42	Q × R	Q × Q ch
43	K × Q	K × R (17)
44	K—B 3	K—K 3
45	K—Q 4	P—R 3
46	P—R 4	P—Kt 4
47	P—R 5	P—Kt 5
48	P—Kt 3	P—Kt 6
49	K—B 3	K × P
50	K × P	K—Q 5
51	K—B 2	K—K 6
52	K—Q 1	K—Q 6
	Resigns	

(1) If 4.., P—K R 3, then 5 B × Kt and not 5 B—R 4 on account of 5.., B—Kt 5 ch, followed by 6.., P × P.

(2) A whim. The customary continuation 5 Kt—B 3 is much superior.

(3) Black plays, as is often done in this opening, to isolate the Queen's Pawn. This procedure has its disadvantages as well as its advantages.

(4) Not fearing 16.., Kt—R 4, having considered an adequate defence.

(5) If 17.., Q Kt—B 3 then simply 18 Q—K 5, etc.

(6) Up to this point the British champion has ably conducted the defence and has secured at least an equal position ; the move adopted, however, allows White to immobilise the Queen besides creating other serious difficulties. Much better would have been 21.., K R—B 1, and if 22 Q Kt—K 5, then 22.., Q—Kt 6, etc.

(7) White now threatens 25 Q—Q 3 followed by 26 P—K Kt 4, etc. This threat induces Black to start on a risky enterprise.

(8) A defence foreseen for some time past and one which forces Black, so as not to take back the Knight (in which case White would play 26 P—B 3, and if 26.., P—K Kt 4 then 27 K Kt—Kt 6 !, etc.) to weaken his King's position seriously.

(9) The only reply ; but it answers the purpose. Fatal would have been 27 R—Q 4 instead on account of 27.., R—B 8 ! !

(10) Black's position was not yet lost, but this move and the next lack boldness and exactitude. Much better would have been here 30.., Q × P, and if 31 Q—R 7 ch, K—B 1 ; 32 Q × R P ch, Q—Kt 2 ; 33 Q—Q 2, then 33.., R—Q 2, with many defensive resources.

(11) Here again 31.., Q × Kt P or even 31.., Q—Kt 2 was indicated. The text-move should have lost off-hand.

(12) In this position White had only to play 33 B—Kt 6 and after 33.., Q—K 6 ch ; 34 R—B 2. The only resource left to Black is the giving up of the Queen for Rook and Bishop, leading to a palpable loss. The sacrifice of the Exchange in the text in order to prevent the pin of the Rook after Q —K 6 ch. Burn gives in *The Field* two interesting variations as follow : 33 B —Kt6, Q—K 6 ch ; 34 R—B 2, K—K 1 ; 35 B × P ch, K—Q 2 ; 36 R × B ch, P × R ; 37 B × P dis ch, K—K 1 ; 38 Q—Kt 8 ch, K moves ; 39 Q—B 7 ch, K—Q 1 ; 40 Q—B 8 ch, K—Q 2 ; 41 P—K 6 ch and wins. If instead 35.., K—Q 1 ; 36 Q—Kt 8 ch, K—K 2 (not 36.., K—Q 2 because of 37 B × P ch) ; 37 Q—Kt 7 and wins. If instead 34.., P—B 4 then 35 Q—R 8 ch, K—K 2 ; 36 Q —Kt 7 ch K—Q 1 ; 37 Q—B 8 ch, K—Q 2 ; 38 Q—Q 6 mate.

(13) A gross blunder ! and one which changes a win into a loss. The win— not a very complicated one—was as follows : 35 Q—Kt 8 ch, K—Q 2 ; 36 Q × P ch, K—B 3 ; 37 Q—K 6 ch, K—Kt 2 ; 38 Q × Q P ch, K—Kt 1 ; 39 B—K 4, R—B 3 ; 40 P—Kt 4, P—R 3 ; 41 P—R 4, etc. The moves which now follow are played with great exactitude by Mr. Yates.

(14) Despairing ! I had forgotten when I played my previous move that after 36 R—B 1 dis ch, K—Q 1 ; 37 Q—Kt 7 ch, Black's King goes *via* B 2 into safety at Kt 1 and that the Rook on B 8 is defended by the Queen. Now follows the agony !

(15) If 41 K—Kt 3 then simply follows 41.., Q × R winning.

(16) Simple and effective.

(17) The Pawn ending which follows is without hope for White and he might have resigned at once.

Game 11. BOGOLJUBOW *v.* THOMAS.

Ruy Lopez (Morphy Defence).

BOGOLJUBOW	THOMAS	BOGOLJUBOW	THOMAS
1 P—K 4	P—K 4	11 O—O—O (4)	B—K 3
2 Kt—K B 3	Kt—Q B 3	12 P—K R 3	Q—Kt 1
3 B—Kt 5	P—Q R 3	13 P—K Kt 4	Q—Kt 5 (5)
4 B—R 4	P—Q 3 (1)	14 B × B	K × B (6)
5 B × Kt ch	P × B	15 P—R 3	Q—Kt 3
6 P—Q 4	P—B 3 (2)	16 Kt—K 2 (7)	Q R—Kt 1
7 Kt—B 3	P—Kt 3	17 Q—B 3	R—Kt 2
8 B—K 3	B—K Kt 2	18 Kt—K 1	Q—Kt 4 (8)
9 Q—Q 2	Kt—K 2	19 Kt—Q 3	Q—B 5
10 B—R 6	O—O (3)	20 P—B 4 (9)	Q × Q

21	P×Q	P×B P
22	Q Kt×P	B—Kt 1
23	P—K R 4	R—Kt 4 (10)
24	K—Q 2	P—Q R 4
25	P—R 4	Q R—Kt 1
26	P—R 5	Kt—B 1 (11)
27	P×P	P×P
28	R—R 2 (12)	R—K 1
29	Kt—B 2	P—Q 4 (13)
30	P×P	P×P
31	P—Kt 5 (14)	P×P
32	Q Kt—Q 3	Kt—Kt 3
33	Kt—K 5 (15)	P—B 4
34	K Kt—Q 3	P×P
35	P×P	Kt—B 5 ch
36	Kt×Kt	P×Kt
37	Kt—K 5	R—Kt 5
38	R—K Kt 1	P—Kt 5 (16)

Position after 38 R—K Kt 1.

39	K R—Kt 2 (17)	B—K 3
40	Kt×P (Kt 4)	P—B 6 ch (18)
41	K×P	R—B 1 ch
42	K—Q 2	R×Q P ch
43	K—B 1	R×P
44	Kt—K 3	R—R 8 ch
45	K—Kt 2	R×R
46	R×R	R—B 4 (19)
47	R—Kt 3	P—Kt 4
48	P—B 4	K—Kt 3
49	K—B 3	R—B 1
50	K—Q 4	P—R 5
51	R—Kt 1	R—Q 1 ch
52	K—B 3	R—Q Kt 1
53	R—Q R 1	R—Q R 1
54	R—R 3	K—B 3 (20)
55	K—Q 4	R—R 4 (21)
56	K—K 4	K—Kt 3
57	K—Q 4	B—Q 2
58	K—B 3	K—B 3
59	K—Q 4	B—B 3
60	P—B 5 (22)	R—R 1 (23)
61	Kt—Q 5 ch	B×Kt (24)
62	K×B	R—R 3 (25)
63	P—B 6	K—K 2 (26)
64	K—B 5	K—Q 1
65	K—Q 6	P—Kt 5
66	R—K Kt 3	P—R 6
67	R×Kt P	K—K 1
68	R—K 4 ch	K—Q 1
69	R—K R 4	K—K 1
70	R—R 8 ch	K—B 2
71	R—R 7 ch	K—K 1
72	K—B 5 (27)	P—R 7 (28)
73	P—B 7	R—R 4 ch
74	K—Kt 6	R—R 3 ch
75	K—B 5	R—R 4 ch
76	K—B 6	R—R 3 ch
77	K—Q 5	R—R 4 ch
78	K—K 6	R—R 3 ch (29)

Draw agreed to.

(1) A defence rarely played, against which the correct reply is 5 P—Q 4, reserving the exchange of Bishop for Knight until having forced the opposition to abandon the centre.

(2) Black can now keep the centre in this way, for the weakening of the diagonal (Q R 2—Kt 8) after the disappearance of White's King's Bishop, is no longer dangerous.

(3) Black has now a very compact arrangement of Pawns. His King's position is, so to say, invulnerable and the open Knight's file provides possibility of counter attack. In short Black already has the better game.

(4) Bogoljubow is going all out, but if he Castled King's side he would be giving up the scanty chance of a King's side attack, while the defects in position would remain the same.

(5) Black gets there first. Not surprising considering the open file. White already must be thinking of defensive moves.

(6) Of course not 14.., Q R—Kt 1 because of 15 Q—R 6, etc.

(7) Probably 16 Q R—Kt 1, Q R—Kt 1 ; 17 Kt—Q 1, etc., was somewhat better, for after the text-move Black will easily be able to force the exchange of Queens, leading to an end-game rather in his favour.

(8) This move reveals a profound judgment of position. Black observes that White has in view the consolidation of his position by 19 Kt—Q 3, after which he could resume his aggressive plans beginning with 20 P—B 4, etc. Hence the necessity of forcing the exchange of Queens, the object attained by the text-move.

(9) It was by no means judicious to weaken still more the position of the Pawns, but even after 20 Q×Q, B×Q ; 21 P—B 4, P×Q P ; 22 Kt×P, P—Q B 4, Black would still have an advantage.

(10) Played in order to prevent 24 P—Kt 5 and with the object of inducing White to weaken himself still more by 24 P—R 4.

(11) The Knight is aiming for Q B 5.

(12) White does not seem to think of any possible action in the centre by Black, otherwise surely he would play 28 Q R—K Kt 1 with the threat of 29 P—Kt 5, which would have forced Black in his turn to make some defensive moves.

(13) This forces an advantageous exchange, for 30 R—K 1 would be immediately bad on account of 30.., Kt—Q 3, etc.

(14) The only means of preventing the entry of the Black Knight into Q B 5.

(15) The position of the Knight gives White some equivalent for the Pawn offered.

(16) A pretty stroke. If 39 R×P Black would gain advantage by 39.., R×Kt, followed by 40.., P—B 6 ch, etc., and after 39 Kt×P (Kt 4) Black would maintain his superiority by 39.., B—K 3 ; 40 Kt—K 5, B—B 4 (with the threat of 41.., P—B 6 ch) ; 41 K—B 3, R×P, etc.

(17) Neither is this move any better.

(18) By this manoeuvre, prepared for a long time, Black definitely secured the advantage of a Pawn. Sir G. Thomas plays this game, as the majority in this tournament, like a master, and it is only lack of technique in finishing which prevented him from taking a much higher place.

(19) In spite of the very restricted material Black still retains winning chances, thanks to the superiority of his Bishop over White's Knight, which latter has no central squares on which to establish itself.

(20) By a series of finely executed manoeuvres Black has succeeded in immobilising the adverse Rook by means of the passed Pawn. White cannot now afford to win the Rook's Pawn by exchanging Rooks, as he would not then have time to sacrifice his Knight for the Knight's Pawn. The end is extremely difficult and is full of finesse.

(21) It was important to prevent 56 K—B 5 followed by 57 K—Kt 6, etc.

(22) Otherwise Black will play 60.., K—K 3, followed by 61.., R—K 4, etc.

(23) A regrettable error which at one stroke loses all the advantage built up by exemplary play to this point. 60.., R—R 2 should have been played in order to enable the King after 61 Kt—Q 5 ch to play to B 4 without being subject to a further check from the Knight at K 7, after which a win would have been relatively easy.

(24) The unfortunate position of the Rook now forces the Exchange, after which the normal result should be a draw.

(25) Black always seems to have the advantage, otherwise the most simple course to secure the draw was 62.., P—Kt 5 ; 63 K—B 6, R—B 1 ch ; 64 K—Kt 6, K—B 4 ; 65 R×P, P—Kt 6, etc.

(26) All this is very complicated and useless but still far from fatal.

(27) An attempt to win, but harmless had Black replied 72.., K—Q 1. What follows is a comedy of errors.

(28) This ill-considered move should have lost the game.

(29) White here proposed a draw, overlooking that he could have won by 79 K—Q 5, R—R 4 ch ; 80 K—B 4, R—R 5 ch ; 81 K—Kt 3, R—R 6 ch ; 82 K—B 2, R—B 6 ch ; 83 K—Kt 2, and Black having no move must abandon his Pawn after which the King approaches the Pawn and wins. However, a win for White would have been a matter of luck, and a draw is a satisfactory conclusion.

Game 12.   RUBINSTEIN *v.* TARRASCH.

Queen's Pawn Opening (Dutch Defence)

	RUBINSTEIN	TARRASCH		RUBINSTEIN	TARRASCH
1	P—Q 4	P—K 3	25	P—K 5 (13)	Q R—Kt 1
2	P—Q B 4	P—K B 4	26	Q × P ch	K—Kt 1
3	P—K Kt 3	P—B 4 (1)	27	Q—Kt 5 ch	K—B 2 (14)
4	Kt—K B 3	P × P	28	B—B 3	R—Kt 1 (15)
5	Kt × P	Kt—K B 3	29	Q—R 5 ch	K—Kt 2
6	B—Kt 2	Kt—B 3	30	B—K 4	Q × P
7	O—O	B—B 4	31	Q × P ch	K—B 1
8	P—K 3 (2)	O—O	32	Q × B	Q × B
9	Kt—Q B 3	P—Q R 3	33	B—R 6 ch	Resigns (16)
10	P—Q R 3 (3)	Q—B 2			
11	P—Q Kt 4	B—K 2			
12	B—Kt 2	Kt—K 4 (4)			
13	P—B 5	Kt—B 5			

(see diagram)

14	Kt × B P (5)	B × P
15	P × B	Q × B P (6)
16	Kt—R 6 ch	P × Kt
17	B—B 1	Q—K 4 (7)
18	Q—Q 3	Q—Q B 4 (8)
19	P—Q R 4 (9)	P—Q 3
20	P—K 4	K—Kt 2 (10)
21	Kt—Q 1 (11)	B—Q 2
22	Kt—K 3	P—Kt 4
23	Kt × Kt	P × Kt
24	Q—Q 2 (12)	Kt—K 1

Position after 13.., Kt—B 5.

(1) A premature move which in any case creates a weakness on the Queen's file. The correct move is 3.., Kt—K B 3 followed by 4.., B—Kt 5 ch as in my game with Bogoljubow.

(2) Quite right. The Queen's Bishop is to be developed with advantage on Kt 2.

(3) Here I should have played 10 P—Kt 3 followed by 11 B—Kt 2 in order to give Black not a shadow of a chance on the Queen's Bishop's file—but latterly Rubinstein has a style much more aggressive than mine.

(4) Black cannot have suspected the ingenious combination initiated by White's 14th move, otherwise he would certainly have played 12.., P—Q 3 and 13.., B—Q 2.

(5) Very pretty and rather deep, for Black temporarily wins a Pawn—but at the expense of jeopardising his King. It is evident that the Knight cannot be taken with advantage on account of 15 Q—Kt 3, etc. If 14.., Kt × B then 15 Kt × B ch, King moves; 16 Q—K 2 and Black's Knight is lost.

(6) Now White has two pieces *en prise* and must lose one. Rubinstein conducts the ensuing attack in a manner worthy of all praise.

(7) A very serious loss of time as a result of which Black's difficulties become insurmountable. The correct line of play was 17.., R—Kt 1; 18 P—K 4, P—K R 4 holding temporarily to the extra Pawn, so as to sacrifice it later in case of necessity. 17.., P—Q 3 also is better then the text.

(8) Still worse would have been 18.., P—Q 4 because of 19 P—K 4.

(9) Not P—K 4 immediately because of 19.., P—Kt 4. Besides that the importance of the square Q R 3 for the Bishop will in the sequel be shown in startling fashion.

(10) To 20.., Kt—Kt 5 White would probably also have replied 21 Kt—Q 1 followed by 22 P—R 3, etc., but in any case it was by no means judicious to place the King on the long diagonal, so easily accessible to White's Bishop.

(11) Rubinstein's plan is simple but irresistible, he means to displace Black's only well-placed piece (the Knight on B 5) after which Black's game will speedily become hopeless.

(12) Already the double threat 25 Q × P ch and 25 B—Q R 3 forcibly regains the Pawn. Oh if that were all ! !

(13) Taking advantage of the fact that Black cannot play 25.., P—Q 4 because of 26 Q × P ch followed by 27 B—Q R 3 winning.

(14) Forced. For if 27.., K—R 1 ; 28 Q—K 7 wins a piece.

(15) And if 28.., Kt—Kt 2, White wins the exchange by 29 B—R 3. There is evidently nothing else to do.

(16) This move gains a Rook after 33.., Kt—Kt 2 ; 34 B × Kt ch, R × B ; 35 Q × P ch, etc.

ROUND V

Game 13.   ALEKHINE *v.* BOGOLJUBOW.

Queen's Gambit Declined.

ALEKHINE	BOGOLJUBOW
1 P—Q 4	P—Q 4
2 Kt—K B 3	Kt—K B 3
3 P—B 4	P—K 3
4 Kt—B 3	Q Kt—Q 2
5 B—Kt 5	B—K 2
6 P—K 3	O—O
7 R—B 1	P—Q R 3 (1)
8 P—B 5	P—B 3
9 P—Q Kt 4	Kt—K 5
10 B—K B 4 (2)	P—K Kt 4 (3)
11 B—Kt 3	Kt × B
12 R P × Kt	P—B 4 (4)

(see diagram)

ALEKHINE	BOGOLJUBOW
13 P—Kt 4	P × P
14 Kt—K 5	Kt × Kt
15 P × Kt	Q—B 2
16 Q—Q 4	R—B 4 (5)
17 B—Q 3	Q × P (6)
18 Q × Q	R × Q
19 R × P (7)	B—B 3 (8)
20 K—Q 2	B—Kt 2

Position after 12.., P—B 4.

ALEKHINE	BOGOLJUBOW
21 Q R—K R 1 (9)	R—Kt 1
22 Kt—R 4	R—B 4 (10)
23 B × R	P × B
24 K R—R 5	B—K 3 (11)
25 R × P	P—Q 5 (12)

26 P×P	R—Q 1	40 P—B 7	K—Q 3 (19)
27 K—B 3 (13)	K—B 1 (14)	41 P—B 8=Q	B×Q
28 R—Q 1	K—B 2	42 Kt×B ch	K—Q 2 (20)
29 Kt—Kt 6 (15)	R—K R 1 (16)	43 R—Q B 1	R—R 7
30 R×B ch	K×R	44 R—B 2	K—K 3
31 P—R 4	R—R 7	45 R—K 2 ch	K—B 3
32 R—K Kt 1	P—B 5	46 Kt—Kt 6	R—R 8
33 P—Q 5 (17)	P×P	47 Kt×P ch	K—Kt 4
34 K—Q 4	P—Kt 6 (18)	48 K—K 5	R—R 1
35 P—B 3	K—B 3	49 Kt×P	R—R 1
36 P—Kt 5	P×P	50 Kt—K 6 ch	K—R 5
37 P×P	R—R 4	51 R—K 1	R—R 1
38 P—B 6	P×P	52 R—R 1 mate	
39 P×P	K—K 2		

(1) This move is justly considered inferior. White is now able to cramp Black's game; relatively better is 7.., P—B 3.

(2) Best, as each exchange of pieces would relieve Black's position.

(3) Bold but risky play well in keeping with Bogoljubow's style. At all costs he wishes to get rid of the dangerous Bishop.

(4) Black now threatens to cramp White's position as well as to repel the attack; for example, 13 Kt—K 5, Kt×Kt; 14 Q—R 5, R—B 2; 15 P×Kt, P—Kt 5, with a defensible position. White's next move frustrates this plan.

(5) The logical continuation; any other move enables White to obtain the advantage as follows: 17 B—K 2, followed by 18 B×P and 19 P—B 4.

(6) Black evidently hopes for 18 B×R, Q×B with two Pawns for the Exchange and good attacking chances.

(7) Black is now a Pawn to the good, but his pieces are so badly placed that he is bound to suffer loss of material during the course of subsequent play.

(8) The only move; if 19.., B—B 1 then 20 R—Q B 7, followed by 21 Kt—R 4 winning.

(9) Preventing the development of the Queen's Bishop, for if 21.., B—Q 2 then evidently 22 R×B ch, followed by 23 R—R 7 ch, etc.

(10) The only means of ultimately enabling the development of the Queen's side. In spite of the gain of the Exchange White would still encounter some difficulty in turning this advantage to account.

(11) The Knight's Pawn cannot be defended if 24.., B—B 3; 25 R—R 6, B—Kt 2 (or 25.., K—Kt 2; 26 R×B followed by 27 R—R 8, etc.); 26 R—Kt 6, etc.

(12) The best move; opening important diagonals for the Bishops and obtaining for the moment the initiative.

(13) Not 27 K—K 3 on account of 27.., P—B 5 ch, etc.

(14) If 27.., K—B 2 at once then 28 R—R 7, etc.

(15) White offers to give back the Exchange in return for a manifestly superior end-game.

(16) Threatening 30.., B—B 3.

(17) By this means which was unavoidable, White obtains a passed Pawn which eventually costs Black a piece.

(18) Black would have a better chance by 34.., P—B 6 which would have freed his Rook.

(19) There is now nothing left if 40.., R—R 1; 41 R—Q B 1, B—B 1; 42 Kt×B ch, R×Kt; 43 K×P and wins.

(20) Black could safely resign here but preferred to play until mated.

Game 14.   TARRASCH *v.* YATES.

Four Knights' Game (*Double Ruy Lopez*).

	TARRASCH	YATES		TARRASCH	YATES
1	P—K 4	P—K 4	45	R—Q 7 ch	K—B 3
2	Kt—K B 3	Kt—Q B 3	46	R×R P	R—B 4
3	Kt—B 3	Kt—B 3	47	R—R 6 ch	K—B 2
4	B—Kt 5	B—Kt 5	48	P—K R 4	R—B 5
5	O—O	O—O	49	P—R 4	R—B 8 (22)
6	P—Q 3	P—Q 3	50	P—R 5 (23)	R—Q R 8
7	B—Kt 5	Kt—K 2 (1)	51	K—B 5	K—K 2
8	Kt—K R 4	P—B 3	52	K×P (24)	K—B 2
9	B—Q B 4	P—Q 4	53	K—B 5	R—R 7
10	B—Kt 3 (2)	Q—Q 3	54	R—R 7 ch	K—Kt 1
11	P—K R 3	P—K R 3	55	P—R 6	R—R 8
12	B×Kt	Q×B	56	P—B 4	R—R 7
13	Q—R 5	B×Kt (3)	57	K—K 5	R—R 4 ch
14	P×B	K—R 2 (4)	58	K—K 6	R—R 5 (25)
15	Kt—B 3 (5)	Kt—Kt 3 (6)	59	P—B 5	R—K 5 ch
16	P×P	P×P	60	K—Q 5	R—R 5
17	B×P	Q—Q 1 (7)	61	P—B 6	K—B 1 (26)
18	B—Kt 3	P—B 4 (8)	62	K—K 6	R—K 5 ch
19	Q R—K 1	Q—B 3	63	K—B 5	R—R 5
20	P—Kt 3 (9)	B—Q 2	64	K—Kt 6	P×P
21	Kt—R 4 (10)	Kt×Kt (11)	65	K×B P	K—Kt 1
22	Q×Kt	Q×Q	66	K—Kt 6	R—Kt 5 ch
23	P×Q (12)	K R—K 1	67	K×P	R—R 5
24	B—Q 5	Q R—B 1	68	K—Kt 6	R—Kt 5 ch
25	P—Q B 4	P—Q Kt 4 (13)	69	K—B 5	R—R 5
26	R—K 2	P×P	70	K—K 6	R—R 8
27	B×P	K—Kt 3 (14)	71	R—R 8 ch	K—R 2
28	R—Kt 1	B—B 3	72	K—Q 6	Resigns
29	R—Kt 3	B—R 1 (15)			
30	R—Kt 5	K—B 3			
31	B—Q 5 (16)	B×B			

(see diagram)

	TARRASCH	YATES
32	R×B	R—K 2
33	R—Q 6 ch	K—B 2
34	P—Q B 4	R—B 4
35	P—B 3 (17)	R—R 4 (18)
36	R—Q B 2	R—Kt 2
37	P—Q 4 (19)	P×P
38	R×Q P	R—R 6
39	K—Kt 2	R—B 2
40	P—R 5 (20)	R—B 4
41	K—Kt 3	R—R 5
42	R—Q 5 (21)	P—B 5 ch
43	K—Kt 4	K R×P
44	R×R	R×R

Position after 31 B—Q 5.

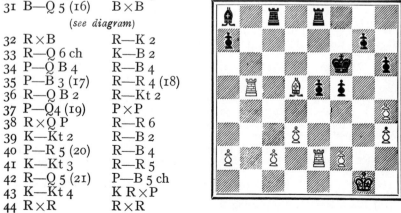

(1) This old-fashioned defence is rightly considered inferior to 7.., B×Kt, followed by 8.., Q—K 2 as in the Bogoljubow—Rubinstein game.

(2) An error which allows Black to obtain at least equality . White should first play 10 B×Kt, retaining the superior game with the chance of a King's side attack.

(3) An unfortunate manoeuvre which ultimately leaves White with an advantage. The correct move was 13.., P—Q 5 and if 14 Kt—K 2, K—R 2 ; 15 Kt—K B 3, B—Q 3, etc., rather in favour of Black.

(4) Relatively better was 14.., P×P, followed by 15.., K—R 2, etc. Although in this case White would have been able to take possession of the Queen's file after 16 Kt—B 3, Kt—Kt 3 ; 17 Q R—Q 1, etc. After the text move Black has to submit to the sacrifice of a Pawn.

(5) If now 15.., P×P, then 16 Kt×P, P—K Kt 3 ; 17 Kt—Kt 4, etc., with obviously the better game.

(6) The attack which Black obtains by this sacrifice is parried in masterly fashion by Dr. Tarrasch.

(7) If 17.., Kt—B 5, then naturally 18 B—K 4 ch, etc.

(8) With the threat 19.., Kt—B 5 ; 20 Q—R 4, P—K Kt4 ; 21 Q—Kt 3, Kt—K 7 ch, a threat which is parried by the following White move.

(9) This move and the following completely destroy Black's hopes.

(10) Quite correct as the winning advantage of White is on the Queen's side ì he does not fear the weakening of the Pawn array on the other side.

(11) There is nothing better, for if 21.., Kt—K 2, then 22 P—K B 4.

(12) Black has now an additional weakness in the centre.

(13) Somewhat better would have been 25.., P—Q Kt 3 for the opening of the Queen's Knight's file must be wholly to White's advantage.

(14) In order to protect the King's Pawn, but the storm breaks from another quarter.

(15) A somewhat mysterious move. Relatively a " neck or nothing " attack offered more chance, *e.g.*, 29.., B—B 6 followed by 30.., P—K 5, etc.

(16) The Rook ending which results from this exchange is only won with great difficulty, but there is no other way to make use of the extra Pawn on the Queen's side.

(17) This move endangered the win. The proper move was 35 R—B 2 preventing 35.., P—K 5 and retaining good chance of winning.

(18) After this weak move White is forced to realise his advantage in material but by playing 35.., P—K 5 Black might force many exchanges leading to a draw, *e.g.*, 36 B P×P, P×P ; 37 P×P, R×B P ; 38 P—K 5, R×R P, etc., or 37 R—B 2 ch, K—K 1 ; 38 R—B 2, P×P ; 39 R×Q P, R—K 5, etc. In both cases the result is evident.

(19) This exchange is indispensable in order to utilise two Rooks for the defence of the Pawns. From this point Dr. Tarrasch plays the end-game in irreproachable style.

(20) This doubled Pawn begins to play a very important part. After the exchange of Rooks Black will no longer be in a position to defend his Bishop's Pawn.

(21) Decisive. For after 42.., K R×P (best) ; 43 R×R, R×R ; 44 R—Q 7 ch, K—B 3 ; 45 R×R P, White would win. Black's next move makes it still more easy for White to win.

(22) The Pawn cannot be defended for if 49.., R—Q 5, then 50 P—R 5, R—R 5 ; 51 K—B 5 followed by 52 R—R 7 ch, etc.

(23) For the same reason White is in no hurry to take it and prefers to reinforce the position still further.

(24) Just at the right moment for if 52.., R—R 5 ch ; 53 K—B 5, R×P ; 54 K—Kt 6 and wins. Now with two Pawns up the rest is only a question of technique.

(25) If 58.., R×K R P then 59 R—Kt 7, R—R 4 ; 60 P—R 7, K—R 2 ; 61 P—B 5 and wins.

(26) Black is evidently playing for stalemate.

Game 15.   THOMAS *v.* RUBINSTEIN.

Ruy Lopez (Morphy Defence).

THOMAS	RUBINSTEIN	THOMAS	RUBINSTEIN
1 P—K 4	P—K 4	30 R×R	R—R 1 (11)

Position after 30.., R—R 1.

THOMAS	RUBINSTEIN	THOMAS	RUBINSTEIN
2 Kt—K B 3	Kt—Q B 3		
3 B—Kt 5	P—Q R 3		
4 B—R 4	Kt—B 3		
5 Q—K 2	P—Q Kt 4		
6 B—Kt 3	B—B 4 (1)		
7 P—B 3	O—O		
8 O—O	P—Q 3		
9 P—Q 3	Kt—K 2 (2)		
10 B—Kt 5 (3)	Kt—Kt 3		
11 Kt—R 4	Kt×Kt		
12 B×Q Kt	P—R 3 (4)		
13 K—R 1	P—Kt 4		
14 B—Kt 3	K—Kt 2		
15 Kt—Q 2	Q—K 2		
16 B—B 2 (5)	B—Q 2		
17 K R—K 1	Q R—K 1 (6)		
18 P—Q R 4 (7)	K R—R 1		
19 P×P	P×P		
20 Kt—B 1	P—R 4	31 R—Q Kt 1	P—Kt 5 (12)
21 P—B 3	P—R 5	32 B—Kt 3	P—K B 3 (13)
22 B—B 2	B×B	33 P—B 4 (14)	P—K B 4 (15)
23 Q×B	P—K Kt 5 (8)	34 K—Kt 1	P×P
24 P×P	Kt×Kt P	35 R—K B 1 (16)	P—K 6 (17)
25 Q—B 3	P—R 6 (9)	36 Q—B 7 ch	K—R 1
26 P—K Kt 3	Q—Kt 4	37 Q—Q 5	P—B 3
27 Kt—K 3	R—R 1 (10)	38 Q×B P	R—Q B 1
28 Kt×Kt	B×Kt	39 Q—K 4	P—K 7
29 Q—B 2	R×R	40 R—K 1	P—Q 4 (18)
		41 P×P	R—B 8
			Resigns

(1) In my opinion these moves of Black constitute the best defence against White's 5th move, giving Black a level game.

(2) But this is a defective manoeuvre which only succeeds, thanks to the unenterprising play of White. A good move was 9.., K—R 1, so as to be able to reply to 10 B—Kt 5 with 10.., P—R 3, followed by 11.., P—Kt 4, without having to fear the sacrifice of the Knight at K Kt 5.

(3) This Bishop is soon going to be dislodged and will merely serve as an object for Black's attack. The correct move was 10 P—Q 4, P×P; 11 P×P, B—Kt 3; 12 P—K 5, K Kt—Q 4; 13 B—Kt 5 with a superior game. Speaking generally Sir George Thomas plays the whole game without initiative.

(4) The beginning of a persistent attack on the King's side.

(5) An absolutely useless move, for the Bishop was better placed on Kt 3. White should have played 16 K R—K 1, and if 16.., B—Q 2; 17 P—Q 4, P×P; 18 P—K 5, P×K P; 19 B×K P, with the initiative as compensation for the Pawn. In any case White must try to play P—Q 4, for without this diversion in the centre he will be crushed on the King's side.

(6) Having sufficiently provided against P—Q 4, Black absolutely dominates the game.

(7) As will be seen, the opening of the Queen's Rook's file will only help Black, but White has no longer any plausible line. 18 Kt—Kt 3 is probably best.

(8) By this move Black opens a line for his attack whatever happens. For if 24 P—K B 4, P—Kt 6, etc.

(9) If 26 P × P, R × P and as played by White the Pawn at R 6 becomes a formidable factor in the attack.

(10) This manoeuvre and what follows is the result of the 18th move of White, who has himself opened the gates to the enemy.

(11) A first surprise, soon to be followed by many others. If White takes this Rook mate follows in three moves.

(12) If White takes, Black regains immediately by 32.., R—Q Kt 1 and the position of White's Pawns is still further weakened. Besides Black threatens 32.., P × P, followed by 33.., R—R 7, etc.

(13) Very judicious, for 32.., P—K B 4 would be premature on account of 33 B—K 6, etc.

(14) This loses at once. Slightly better was 33 B—Q 5, and if 33.., R—K B 1, then 34 K—Kt 1, P—K B 4 ; 35 P × P, R × P ; 36 Q—K 1 and White could prolong the defence for a little.

(15) From now to the end every move of Black is like the blow of a club·

(16) A move of despair. If 35 P × P, R—K B 1 ; 36 Q—K 1, R—B 6 ; 37 B—Q 1, R—K 6 ; 38 Q—B 2, R × P ; 39 B × B, Q × B ; 40 R—K B 1, R—B 5 winning easily.

(17) The game is of course won in any case, but Rubinstein's style in finishing is truly artistic. The sacrifice of the Bishop's Pawn later gains notable time for the move 39.., P—K 7.

(18) The climax. Either Black gets the square K 6 for the Queen or else the fatal opening of the Bishop's file. A fine game !

ROUND VI

Game 16.   ALEKHINE *v.* RUBINSTEIN.

Queen's Gambit Declined (in effect).

ALEKHINE	RUBINSTEIN
1 P—Q 4	P—Q 4
2 Kt—K B 3	P—Q B 4 (1)
3 P—B 4	P—K 3
4 P × Q P	K P × P
5 Kt—B 3	Kt—Q B 3
6 P × P	P—Q 5
7 Kt—Q R 4	B × P (2)
8 Kt × B	Q—R 4 ch
9 Q—Q 2	Q × Kt
10 P—K 3	P × P
11 Q × P ch	Q × Q ch
12 B × Q	K Kt—K 2
13 B—Q Kt 5	O—O
14 O—O	B—K 3
15 Kt—Q 4	Kt × Kt
16 B × Kt	Kt—B 3
17 B × Kt	P × B

Position after 17.., P × B.

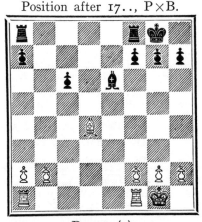

Drawn (3)

Round Six

39

(1) Rubinstein adopts Tarrasch's Defence, the variation of which he has disputed all along and against which he has secured notable successes in a great many games. It will be interesting to see in the future what novelty he has discovered for the defence in the P—K Kt 3 attack, which is almost unanimously considered to demolish Tarrasch's system. In this game I tested the value of another line of play, by some somewhat unkindly dubbed " ca-canny " !

(2) Avoiding the complications arising from 7.., P—Q Kt 4 ! ? ; 8 P×P e.f., P×P ; 9 P—Q Kt 3, the aftermath of which is far from being exhaustively analysed. The text-move gives a slight superiority to White (consisting of two Bishops against Bishop and Knight), but one which is much too small to seek a win against an adversary of Rubinstein's calibre.

(3) It strikes me that no one can reproach the adversaries for having abandoned as drawn a position so sterile and denuded of all interest.

Game 17.   BOGOLJUBOW *v.* YATES.

Queen's Gambit Declined.

BOGOLJUBOW	YATES	BOGOLJUBOW	YATES
1 P—Q 4	P—Q 4	24 Q—B 4	Q R—B 1
2 P—Q B 4	P—K 3	25 Kt—K 5 (8)	P—Q B 4
3 Kt—K B 3	Kt—K B 3	26 Q—R 6	Q—Q 3
4 Kt—B 3	B—K 2		
5 B—Kt 5	O—O		
6 P—K 3	Q Kt—Q 2		
7 R—B 1	P—B 3		
8 Q—B 2	P×P		
9 B×P	Kt—Q 4		
10 B×B	Q×B		
11 O—O	Kt×Kt		
12 Q×Kt	P—Q Kt 3		
13 Q—Q 3 (1)	R—Q 1 (2)		
14 Q—K 2	P—Q R 3 (3)		
15 B—Q 3	B—Kt 2		
16 B—K 4	Q R—B 1		
17 R—B 3 (4)	Kt—B 3		
18 B—Q 3	Kt—Q 4		
19 Q R—B 1	Kt—Kt 5		
20 B—B 4	P—Q R 4 (5)	27 K R—Q 1	R—R 1
21 P—Q R 3	Kt—Q 4	28 Q—Kt 7 (9)	Kt—K 2 (10)
22 B—R 6 (6)	B×B	29 Kt—B 4	Resigns
23 Q×B	R—R 1 (7)		

Position after 26 Q—R 6.

(1) So far this game is a repetition of my game with Capablanca, London, 1922. The Queen move aims at exchange of Bishops which would weaken still further Black's Queen's side.

(2) Capablanca here played 13.., P—Q B 4. The Rook move has little to recommend it, for it shifts the White Queen to a better square.

(3) Avoiding the Exchange but creating a new weakness at Q Kt 3.

(4) Very cunning, threatening 18 Q—B 2. Apparently Black will now gain time by transferring his Knight to Q 4, but in reality the manoeuvre of this piece will not improve his position, for it does not remove the essential weakness of the Queen's side.

(5) Threatening 21.., P—Q Kt 4 and 22.., P—R 5. Moreover, White was threatening to win a Pawn.

(6) And now the object aimed at in his last seven moves is at last attained.

(7) Something had to be done to combat the threat 24 P—K 4.

(8) This forces the reply which gives White a new point of vantage at Q Kt 5.

(9) With the double threat of 29 P—K 4 or 29 P×P, followed by 30 Kt—B 6, etc.

(10) A mistake which loses straight away, but in any case the game could hardly be saved, *e.g.*, 28.., Q—K 2 ; 29 Q×Q, Kt×Q ; 30 Kt—B 4, P×P ; 31 Kt×Kt P and White's position is evidently superior.

Game 18.   THOMAS *v.* TARRASCH.

Queen's Pawn Opening (Dutch Defence).

THOMAS	TARRASCH	THOMAS	TARRASCH
1 P—Q 4	P—K 3	25 B—B 3	Kt—Q 4 (12)
2 P—Q B 4	P—K B 4	26 B—Q 4	R—R 2
3 Kt—Q B 3	Kt—K B 3	27 Q—B 3	P—B 6
4 P—K 3	P—Q Kt 3	28 B×Q B P	Kt×B
5 B—Q 3	B—Kt 2	29 Q×Kt	R×P
6 P—B 3 (1)	P—B 4	30 K R—Q Kt 1	R×R
7 K Kt—K 2	Kt—B 3	31 Q×R (13)	
8 O—O	B—Q 3		Drawn
9 P—Q Kt 3	Q—B 2 (2)		
10 P—B 4	P—Q R 3 (3)	Position after 23.., Q—Kt 4.	
11 P—Q 5	Kt—K 2		
12 P—K 4 (4)	P×K P		
13 Kt×P	P×P		
14 Kt×Kt ch	P×Kt		
15 P×P	B×Q P (5)		
16 Kt—B 3	B—B 2 (6)		
17 B×Q R P (7)	O—O		
18 B—Q 3 (8)	P—B 5		
19 P×P	B×Q B P		
20 Kt—K 4 (9)	B—B 4 ch		
21 Kt×B	Q×Kt ch		
22 K—R 1	P—Q 4		
23 B—Kt 2	Q—Kt 4 (10)		
(see *diagram*)			
24 B×B (11)	P×B		

(1) This old system, recommended by Stein, has the disadvantage of weakening the King's side too soon. Black can reply by 6.., Kt—R 4 practically forcing the exchange of Queens (7 Q—Q 2, Q—R 5 ch ; 8 Q—B 2, etc.), after which he has no longer much to fear and as in the present game obtains a satisfactory game.

(2) Loss of time, of which White takes prompt and clever advantage. The correct move was 9.., Q—Kt 1, and if 10 P—B 4, O—O, etc., with a good game.

(3) If now 10.., O—O; 11 Kt—Kt 5, Q—Kt 1; 12 Kt×B, Q×Kt; 13 B—R 3, with the better game.

(4) A pretty combination which offers a Pawn which is regained on the 17th move with a great advantage in position.

(5) If 15.., Kt×P; 16 B—K 4, Kt—K 6; 17 B×Kt, B×B; 18 Kt—B 3, B—Kt 3; 19 Kt—Q 5, etc.

(6) Otherwise 17 Q—R 5 ch, etc.

(7) The hidden point of the manoeuvre started at the 12th move. Black's game is now very much compromised and he only succeeds in escaping by a chess miracle.

(8) This is not the best. 18 B—B 4, Q—B 3; 19 R—K 1 with the threat 20 Kt—K 4 would have kept the Black pieces in their unfavourable positions and probably won the game. Now Black gets a chance to reply.

(9) Neither does 20 B×B ch, Q×B; 21 Q×B, Q×Kt, etc., lead to anything.

(10) Before this Black should play 23.., R—B 2 for now White could by an elegant sacrifice get a crushing attack.

(11) What a pity! A little more boldness would have won the game, *e.g.*, 24 B×P ch, K×B; 25 Q—R 5 ch, K—Kt 1; 26 R—B 3, B—Q 6; 27 R—K 1 and Black has no defence against the many threats. Or if 26.., R—B 2; 27 R—R 3, K—B 1 (if 27.., R—Kt 2, then 28 B×P); 28 Q—R 8 ch, Kt—Kt 1; 29 R—Kt 3, K—K 2; 30 R—K 1 ch, K—Q 2; 31 R×Kt, wins. Sir George Thomas explained that on his previous move he examined this sacrifice but then it was not sound and he did not at the time appreciate the difference made by the intervening move. On the other hand the exchange of Bishops leads to a level game.

(12) White was threatening 26 P—Q R 4, Q—Q B 4; 27 Q R—Kt 1, etc. Consequently Black prefers to clear off immediately.

(13) Now the forces are so reduced that neither can contemplate victory.

ROUND VII

Game 19.   TARRASCH *v.* ALEKHINE.
Four Knights' Game.

TARRASCH	ALEKHINE	TARRASCH	ALEKHINE
1 P—K 4	P—K 4	17 K R—Q 1 (8)	P—K Kt 4
2 Kt—K B 3	Kt—Q B 3	*(see diagram)*	
3 Kt—B 3	Kt—B 3	18 P—K Kt 3	P—K R 4
4 B—Kt 5	Kt—Q 5 (1)	19 R—Q 2	P—Kt 5
5 Kt×Kt (2)	P×Kt	20 B—Kt 2	P—R 5
6 P—K 5	P×Kt	21 Q R—Q 1	P×P
7 P×Kt	Q×P (3)	22 R P×P	R—R 4 (9)
8 Q P×P	P—B 3	23 P—K B 4 (10)	P—Kt 3
9 B—Q 3	P—Q 4	24 K—B 2	B—B 3
10 O—O	B—K 3	25 P—R 3	K—Kt 2
11 Q—R 5 (4)	B—K 2	26 K—Kt 1 (11)	R—K 1
12 B—K 3	P—B 4 (5)	27 K—B 2	Q R—K R 1
13 B—Kt 5 ch	K—B 1	28 K—B 1 (12)	R—Q 1
14 B—K 2 (6)	P—K R 3	29 K—Kt 1	P—R 4
15 Q—B 3 (7)	Q×Q	30 K—B 2	B—K 2
16 B×Q	R—Q 1	31 K—Kt 1	B—B 3

32	K—B 2	R—Q 2
33	R—K R 1 (13)	R×R
34	B×R	R—Q 1
35	K—B 1	P—Q 5
36	P×P	P×P
37	B—B 2	B—B 5 ch (14)
38	K—K 1 (15)	P—Kt 4
39	K—Q 1	P—Kt 5 (16)
40	P×P	P×P
41	P—Kt 3	B—Q Kt 4
42	B—K 4 (17)	P—Q 6 (18)
43	P×P (18a)	B—B 6
44	R—R 2 (19)	B×P
45	B×B	R×B ch
46	K—K 2	R—B 6
47	R—R 4 (20)	K—Kt 3 (21)
48	R—R 6 ch	P—B 3 (22)
49	R—R 2 (23)	K—B 4
50	R—R 5 ch	K—K 5
51	R—R 8	B—Kt 7
52	R—K 8 ch	K—Q 4
53	R—Q 8 ch	K—K 5
54	R—K 8 ch	K—Q 4
55	R—Q 8 ch	K—B 3

56	R—Q 3	R×R
57	K×R	K—Q 4
58	B—Kt 6	B—R 8
59	B—R 7	B—B 6
60	B—B 2	P—B 4
61	K—K 2	K—K 5 (24)
62	B—B 5	

Drawn

Position after 17 K R—Q 1.

(1) Rubinstein Defence, which I consider sound and leading with ease to equality.

(2) A move I played against Capablanca at St. Petersburg in 1914. This move is simple and presents no complications or difficulties for Black. Burn suggests as an alternative 5 B—R 4, and points out that Schlechter recommended the doubtful continuation 5 Kt×P, Q—K 2 ; 6 Kt—B 3, Kt×B ; 7 Kt×Kt, Q×P ch ; 8 Q—K 2, Q×Q ch ; 9 K×Q, Kt—Q 4 ; 10 P—B 4, P—Q R 3, in which Black would have a slight advantage for the end-game.

(3) The capture of the Queen's Pawn by 7.., P×P ch ; 8 B×P, Q×P ; 9 O—O allows White to develop a formidable attack.

(4) A good move ; threatening 12 B—K Kt 5 and preventing 11.., O—O—O. Black now decides to forego any idea of Castling so as to restrain the power of the Bishops.

(5) Forced in view of the menace of 13 B—Q 4.

(6) The Bishop had to return immediately owing to the threat of 14.., P—B 5, etc. More energetic, however, would have been 14 B—Q 3, followed (for example after 14.., P—K R 3) by 15 P—K B 4.

(7) Now on the contrary 15 P—K B 4 leads to nothing on account of 15.., B—B 4, etc. Already White can only with difficulty avoid the exchange of Queens.

(8) It might appear at first sight that White's game is decidedly preferable owing to the weakness of Black's Queen's Pawn, which can be triply threatened. Black's subsequent manoeuvres, however, puts the position in its true merits.

(9) The key of Black's play ; the Pawn is now definitely protected, and besides this, Black's pieces are now more active than those of his adversary. In spite of this, however, it is difficult to obtain a working superiority.

(10) So as to enable the Queen's Bishop to take part in the King's side defence.

(11) White has now been reduced to a complete standstill.

(12) These moves and some of the subsequent are made to gain time on the clocks. If 28 B × Q P, B × B ; 29 R × B, R × R ; 30 R × R, R—R 7 ch ; 31 K—K 1. An even game.

(13) White would have done better to leave the position intact, as after the exchange of Rooks Black is enabled to force the advance of the Queen's Pawn. *Per contra* had White persisted in marking time, Black in order to try for a win would have had to risk a complicated and difficult plan. For example, the march of the King to the Queen's side in order to strengthen and advance the Pawns all along the line.

(14) This careless move might have lost Black his advantage, whilst 37.., B—B 4 ! followed by 38.., R—Q B 1, etc., would still have maintained a firm grip on the adversary's game.

(15) The correct reply was 38 K—Kt 1 threatening 39 B—K 4 and 40 B—B 5, etc., which would probably have forced Black to adopt the drawing variation, 38..P—Q 6, etc. After the text-move White's position again becomes critical.

(16) Threatening 40.., P—Kt 6, etc.

(17) An unsuccessful attempt to prevent the advance of the Queen's Pawn.

(18) A pretty shot which should have forced the win.

(18a) Or else 43 B × P, B—B 6 ; 44 R—K 2, B × B ; 45 P × B, R × P ch ; 46 K—B 2, R—B 6 ; 47 K moves, B—B 3 and wins.

(19) The sacrifice of the Exchange was not good enough, for example 44 B—Q B 5, B × R ; 45 K × B, P—B 4 !, etc.

(20) It is easy to see that all White's pieces are now tied up. If the Rook moves the Bishop comes back to B 3 and the Queen's Knight's Pawn is lost. All that is now necessary is to induce this Rook move, which is done by White moving his King as follows : 47.., K—R 2 ! and the game is easily won. If 48 R—R 7 ?, R × B ch, etc. Instead of this simple move Black makes a mistake and allows White to escape with a draw.

(21) 47.., K—R 2 would have won a Pawn as White must move either the Rook or Bishop.

(22) There is now nothing left. If now 48.., K—Kt 2 (or R 2) White forces the draw as follows : 49 R—Q 6, etc., and if 48.., K—B 4 ; 49 R—R 4 ! and Black cannot now gain sufficient time for if 49.., K—K 5 ; 50 R—R 8 !, etc

(23) Simpler would have been 49 R—K 6 followed by 50 R—K 3.

(24) A last hope, if 62 B—K 3, B—K 8 and wins.

Game 20.   THOMAS *v.* YATES.

Ruy Lopez (Berlin Defence).

THOMAS	YATES	THOMAS	YATES
1 P—K 4	P—K 4	9 B × Kt	Kt P × B (3)
2 Kt—K B 3	Kt—Q B 3	10 Kt × P (4)	P—Q 3 (5)
3 B—Kt 5	Kt—B 3	11 Kt × P	Q—Q 2
4 P—Q 4 (1)	P × P	*(see diagram)*	
5 O—O	B—K 2	12 Q—B 4 ch	R—B 2 (6)
6 Q—K 2	O—O	13 P—K 6 (7)	Q × P
7 P—K 5	Kt—K 1	14 Q × Q	B × Q
8 R—Q 1	P—B 3 (2)	15 R—K 1	B—Q 2

16	Kt×B ch	K—B 1	Position after 11.., Q—Q 2.
17	Kt—Q 5	P—B 3	
18	Kt—K 3	P—Q 4	
19	P—Q Kt 3	P—K B 4	
20	P—K B 3 (8)	Kt—B 3	
21	Kt—B 1	P—K R 3	
22	Kt—B 3	P—Kt 4	
23	P—Kt 3	K—Kt 2	
24	Kt—R 4	R—K Kt 1	
25	Kt—B 5	B—B 1	
26	B—Kt 2	P—K R 4	
27	R—K 2	P—B 5	
28	Q R—K 1	P—Kt 5	
29	Kt—K 6 ch	K—R 2	
30	Kt×P	P×P	
31	R—K 7	Resigns	

(1) A variation not much played and which, for this reason has a chance of success against a player who does not know it sufficiently well. With correct play on both sides it only leads to equality.

(2) A fatal mistake at the 8th move! The proper move was 8.., P—Q 4 and if 9 B×Kt, P×B; 10 Kt×P, Q—Q 2 Black will have a satisfactory game thus: 11 Kt—Q B 3, P—Q B 4; 12 Kt—Kt 3, P—Q B 3; 13 Kt—R 4, P—B 5; 14 K Kt—B 5, Q—B 4; 15 P—Q Kt 3, P×P; 16 R P×P, as suggested by Mr. Burn in *The Field*. The way in which White now forces the win gives the game a value in the theory of chess.

(3) If 9.., Q P×B, then 10 R×P, B—Q 2; 11 P—K 6 winning.

(4) Threatening to win the Queen by 11 Kt×P. Moreover 11 Kt—K 6 would have possibilities.

(5) Somewhat better would have been 10.., P—Q 4 which only loses two Pawns, whereas now Black loses a piece. 10.., P—Q 4; 11 Kt×P, Q—Q 2; 12 Kt×B ch, Q×Kt; 13 R×P is the alternative.

(6) The consequences of 12.., K—R 1 would have been the same.

(7) This move clearly wins a piece and the game—the rest might be passed over in silence.

(8) This move and a few following give the impression of having been made under time pressure.

Game 21.   Rubinstein *v.* Bogoljubow.
Queen's Gambit Declined.

RUBINSTEIN	BOGOLJUBOW	RUBINSTEIN	BOGOLJUBOW
1 P—Q 4	P—Q 4	13 B×Kt	Q×B ch
2 P—Q B 4	P—Q B 3	14 K—Kt 2	Q—K 5 ch (9)
3 P—K 3 (1)	Kt—B 3	15 R—B 3	Kt—Kt 3
4 Kt—Q B 3	B—B 4 (2)	16 Kt—B 3	Q—B 4
5 P×P	Kt×P (3)	17 B—Q 3	Q—Q R 4
6 B—B 4	P—K 3	18 P—Q R 3	Kt—Q 2 (10)
7 K Kt—K 2 (4)	Kt—Q 2	19 P—Q Kt 4	Q—Kt 3
8 O—O	Q—R 5 (5)	20 P—Kt 5 (11)	B—K 2
9 P—K 4 (6)	B×P	21 P×P	P×P
10 P—K Kt 3 (7)	Q—Kt 5	22 R—Kt 1 (12)	Q×P
11 Kt×B	Q×Q Kt	23 Q—B 2	R—Q Kt 1 (13)
12 P—B 4 (8)	Kt—K 6	24 R×R ch	Kt×R

25 B×P	P—Kt 3 (14)	29 P×P dis ch	K—K 2
26 B×P	P×B	30 R—B 7 ch (16)	K—Q 1
27 Q×P ch	K—B 1	31 Kt—K 4	Q—Kt 7 ch
28 P—B 5	B—B 4 (15)	32 K—B 3	Q×P ch (17)

Position after 28 P—B 5.

33 K—Kt 4	B—K 2
34 Q—Kt 7	R×P (18)
35 Q—Kt 8 ch	K—B 2
36 Q—B 8 (19)	K—Kt 2
37 Q×B ch	Q×Q
38 R×Q ch	K—Kt 3
39 R—K 8	K—B 2
40 P—K 7	K—Q 2
41 R×Kt	K×P
42 R—Kt 7 ch	K—K 3
43 R×P	K—Q 4
44 K—B 4	P—B 4
45 R—R 5	K—Q 5
46 Kt×P	R—B 7 ch
47 K—Kt 4	Resigns (20)

(1) Rubinstein inaugurates, in this game, a very interesting innovation seeking to avoid the line in which Black retains the gambit Pawn.

(2) This sally of the Bishop is the logical sequel of Black's 2nd move.

(3) If 5.., P×P; 6 Q—Kt 3 with advantage.

(4) This is the point of the innovation. After the development of the Knight at K 2 White threatens at once a strong advance of Pawns in the centre and should, with correct play, obtain in this way the advantage.

(5) An inoffensive reply to which White should simply play 9 P—B 3, and if 9.., B—Q 3; 10 P—K Kt 3 and Black is forced to withdraw his Queen to K 2, for if 10.., Q—R 6; 11 P—K 4, Kt×Kt; 12 P×Kt, B—Kt 3; 13 P—K 5 followed by 14 Kt—B 4 and wins.

(6) A mistake which loses a Pawn for nothing. White had probably only considered the variation 9.., Kt×Kt; 10 Kt×Kt, B×P; 11 P—K Kt 3 and wins.

(7) But Rubinstein is clearly shaken. Why this further weakening of the King's side. 10 Kt×B at once was evidently better.

(8) With the evident threat of 13 B—Q 3.

(9) White again threatens to shut in the Queen by 15 B—Q 3.

(10) From this moment Black begins to show great uncertainty and so allows White to form a dangerous attack. The correct move here was simply 18.., O—O—O, immediately attacking the weak Queen's Pawn. Now the chances for attack are about equal. But Black's advantage in material should have eventually decided the game in his favour.

(11) Preventing Black from Castling.

(12) After the initial mistake Rubinstein plays with great energy right to the end. By the sacrifice of another Pawn he not only gains important time but opens a new line of attack, the force of which is soon to be felt.

(13) Having obtained an advantage of two Pawns Black wishes at all costs to hold it, and this desire finally costs him the game. A wiser move was 23.., P—Kt 3, and if 24 B—K 4, Q—B 4; 25 Q—R 4 (or else 25 R—Kt 7, Kt—B 3), O—O; 26 Q×B P, Q R—Q 1, etc., with some chance of winning, the text move induces White to make a sacrifice which gives at least plenty of chances for a draw.

(14) 25.., Q—B 3 would have been followed by 26 Q—Kt 1 and Q—Kt 7. The capture of the piece offered is in any case very dangerous.

(15) The position is complicated and Black was short of time so he should have been satisfied to force a draw by 28.., Q—Q 7 ch; 29 K—B 1 (29 R—B 2 R×P ch), 29.., Q—B 8 ch; 30 K—Kt 2, etc.

(16) White also misses the best move. 30 P—K R 4 at once provides good winning chances.

(17) This check is a fatal loss of time. 32.., B—K 2 was necessary, followed by 33.., R—K 1 with some chance of defence.

(18) This shortens the struggle, the issue of which was no longer in doubt. Also after 34.., R—K 1; 35 P—R 4, Q—Kt 5; 36 Q—K 5, etc., White wins.

(19) Regains a piece after which the King's Pawn will cost Black another There is nothing else to be done.

(20) A lively and interesting game, in spite of and in a measure perhaps because of the errors on both sides.

ROUND VIII

Game 22.   ALEKHINE *v.* THOMAS.

Queen's Gambit Declined (in effect).

ALEKHINE	THOMAS	ALEKHINE	THOMAS
1 P—Q 4	Kt—K B 3		
2 Kt—K B 3	P—K 3		
3 P—B 4	P—Q 4		
4 Kt—B 3	B—K 2		
5 B—Kt 5	Q Kt—Q 2		
6 P—K 3	O—O		
7 R—B 1	P—B 3		
8 Q—B 2 (1)	P—K R 3 (2)		
9 B—R 4	R—K 1 (3)		
10 B—Q 3	P×P		
11 B×P	Kt—Q 4		
12 B—K Kt 3	Kt×Kt		
13 P×Kt (4)	P—Q Kt 3		
14 O—O	B—Kt 2		
15 K R—Q 1	Q—B 1 (5)		
16 Q—K 2 (6)	P—Q R 4 (7)		
17 B—Q 3 (8)	P—Q Kt 4 (9)	26 P—Q 5	K P×P
18 Kt—Q 2 (10)	Q—Q 1	27 P×P	R×B
19 Q—B 3 (11)	R—R 2	28 P×P	B×P (18)
20 Kt—K 4	Kt—B 3 (12)	29 R×Q (19)	B×R (20)
21 B—K 5 (13)	Kt×Kt	30 Q—B 4	R—K 2 (21)
22 B×Kt	Q—Q 2	31 B—Kt 3	R—R 1
23 P—B 4 (14)	P—Kt 5	32 B—Q 5	R—B 1
24 B—B 2 (15)	B—K B 1	33 R×R	B×R
25 B—R 4 (16)	R—K 2 (17)	34 Q—Kt 8 (22)	B—K 3

Position after 25.., R—K 2.

35 B×B	R×B	48 K—Q 3	R—Q 3 ch
36 Q—Kt 5	R—Q 3	49 K—K 3	R—Q 2
37 P—Kt 3	R—Q 8 ch	50 Q—B 2	R—R 2
38 K—Kt 2	R—Q R 8	51 P—K 5	R—R 3
39 Q—R 4 (23)	B—K 2 (24)	52 K—K 4	R—Kt 3
40 Q×R P (25)	R—Q B 8	53 P—Kt 4	R—Kt 4
41 Q—R 8 ch	B—B 1	54 K—Q 4	R—R 4
42 Q—K 4	R—B 6	55 P—K R 4	R—Kt 4
43 Q—Kt 1 (26)	R—R 6	56 P—R 5	P×P
44 K—B 3	R—R 3	57 P×P	R—Kt 3
45 P—K 4	R—B 3 ch	58 P—B 5	K—Kt 2
46 K—K 2	R—R 3	59 Q—B 7	R—Kt 4
47 P—B 4	P—Kt 3	60 K—B 4	Resigns

(1) What might be termed the classical position. Capablanca here plays 8.., P×P; 9 B×P, Kt—Q 4; 10 B×B, Q×B; 11 O—O, Kt×Kt; 12 Q×Kt, P—Q Kt 3, etc., and considers the position arrived at as satisfactory for Black.

(2) This move should form part of a special plan (for instance, as in Bogoljubow's variation which I adopted against Rubinstein), otherwise it only has the effect of placing the Bishop on more favourable squares.

(3) Now one sees the idea of the previous move; Black does not wish to face after 10 B—Q 3, P×P; 11 B×P, Kt—Q 4 the move 12 Kt—K 4 which I played with success against Yates in London.

(4) Also good would be 13 Q×Kt, Kt—Kt 3; 14 B—Kt 3, Kt—Q 4; 15 Q—Q 3, B—Kt 5 ch; 16 Kt—Q 2, etc.

(5) One of the main difficulties of Black's game consists in finding a good square for the Queen.

(6) Preventing 16.., B—R 3. Furthermore, as a matter of general principle K 2 is usually the best post for the Queen in this opening.

(7) Black still attempts to exchange Bishops.

(8) Which White avoids; if now 17.., B—R 3; 18 P—B 4, etc.

(9) A new plan. Black proposes to establish two Pawns to one on the right wing. Should White advance his Queen's Bishop's Pawn to the fourth, Black counters this by advancing the Queen's Bishop's Pawn only when he judges that the time has come when this advantage will not serve the adversary's purpose.

(10) The advance of the King's Pawn would only end in occupying the centre square so necessary to White's pieces. The Knight now threatens to go to Q 6, forcing its exchange and leaving White two Bishops against Bishop and Knight.

(11) Gaining an important move through the threat of 20 B×P.

(12) Practically forced.

(13) This simple move is far stronger than the seductive looking 21 Kt—B 5, to which Black would most certainly reply by 21.., B—R 1.

(14) The right moment for this advance, as White can immediately fix the Black Pawns on the Queen's side.

(15) The point; if now 24.., P—R 5 then 25 P—B 5, followed by 26 R—Kt 1, and Black cannot defend the Pawn.

(16) After this move, strategically, the game is won.

(17) A desperate move, made in order to weaken the advance P—Q 5. A glance will suffice to show the desperate position of Black's game. White had only to play here 26 Q—Kt 3, first defending the Queen's Bishop, then 27 P—Q 5 and the game was won without complications. The more forcing line adopted should also have led to an easy win.

(18) The only move ; if 28.., Q—K 2 ; then 29 R—Q 7, B×P ; 30 R×Q, B×Q ; 31 R×Q R, R—K Kt 4 ; 32 B—B 6 ! and wins ; if 28.., Q—B 4 ; then 29 Q×Q, R×Q ; 30 P×B, R×Kt P ; 31 R—Q 8 and wins.

(19) An extraordinary error of intention. The obvious 29 R×B, as planned when advancing the Queen's Pawn forced the game in a few moves, for example : 29.., Q—K 2 ; 30 R—B 8, R—B 2 ; 31 R—Kt 8, followed by 32 K R—Q 8, etc. I instantly captured the Queen, thus adding a further three hours' labour to doubts as to the issue of the game. This class of blunder caused through a certain nervousness which I had eliminated from my play a long time ago, returned to me in the course of several of my games at Hastings, and was due to the strain and vicissitudes of the London International.

(20) Not 29.., B×Q, which would have led to the aforementioned variation.

(21) Again best on account of the threat of 31 Q—Q 4.

(22) After this move Black cannot save the Queen's Rook's Pawn. **For** instance, if 34.., B—B 4 ; 35 P—K R 3, followed by 36 Q—Kt 5, etc.

(23) White would at once play 39 Q×R P, P—Kt 6 ; 40 Q—B 3, etc., but tries to have as many Pawns as possible on the board.

(24) Black, on the other hand, should make as many Pawn exchanges as possible so as to free the board and increase the Rook's activity for the end-game which follows. Consequently, the correct move was 39.., R—Q Kt 8 ; 40 Q× R P, P—Kt 6, etc. In any case, as was shown by the other masters at Hastings, White would have succeeded in winning by adopting an analogous method to the one which follows.

(25) Taking advantage of the circumstance that 40.., P—Kt 6 is not feasible owing to 41 Q—K 5 followed by 42 Q—Kt 8 ch, etc.

(26) The Queen is now in an unassailable position and everything is prepared for the decisive advance of the King and Pawns. The end-game which follows is typical of its class and easily understood. The final phase, however, is not without a certain amount of distinctive originality.

Game 23.   YATES *v.* RUBINSTEIN.

Ruy Lopez (Morphy Defence).

	YATES	RUBINSTEIN		YATES	RUBINSTEIN
1	P—K 4	P—K 4	13	Q×B	P×P
2	Kt—K B 3	Kt—Q B 3	14	P×P	Kt—B 5 (5)
3	B—Kt 5	P—Q R 3	15	Kt—Q 2	R—B 1
4	B—R 4	Kt—B 3	16	Kt—B 1 (6)	P—Kt 3 (7)
5	O—O	B—K 2	17	Kt—Kt 3	Kt—K 1
6	R—K 1	P—Q Kt 4	18	Kt—B 5 (8)	B—Kt 4
7	B—Kt 3	P—Q 3		*(see diagram)*	
8	P—B 3	O—O (1)	19	Q—Kt 4	B×B
9	P—Q 4	B—Kt 5	20	Q R×B	Kt—Kt 2 (9)
10	P—Q 5 (2)	Kt—Q R 4	21	Kt×Kt	K×Kt
11	B—B 2	P—B 3 (3)	22	R—Kt 1 (10)	P—B 4
12	P—K R 3 (4)	B×Kt	23	Q—K 2	Q—Kt 4

24	P—Q R 4 (11)	P—K 5
25	P × P	P × P
26	R—R 1	R—K B 2
27	K—R 1 (12)	R—B 4
28	K R—Q 1 (13)	Kt × P
29	K R—Q Kt 1	Kt—B 5
30	R—R 6	R × P (14)
31	R—Q 1	R—K 4
32	B—Kt 3	P—Q 4
33	B × Kt	Kt P × B
34	R—Q 6	P—B 5
35	Q—Q 2	P—K 6
36	Q—K 2	P—B 6
37	P × B P	Q—R 4

Resigns (15)

Position after 18 Kt—B 5.

(1) Probably better than 8.., Kt—Q R 4 for the advance of the White Pawn to Q 4 about to follow is advantageously parried by the pinning of the King's Knight while Black's Queen's Knight remains on B 3.

(2) In any case this advance which allows Black almost immediately to open the Bishop's file is premature. The usual move 10 B—K 3 is preferable.

(3) Rubinstein at once takes advantage of his opponent's strategic error.

(4) After this move Black, by the exchange which follows, creates for himself, future chances in the centre, besides those of the Queen's side. A better move would have been 12 P × P to which Black would probably have replied 12.., R—B 1, etc.

(5) The Knight will remain in this commanding position for many moves, although White had his opportunity to exchange it.

(6) This attempt at attack is very easily met by Black. White would have done better to play for simplification by 16 Kt × Kt followed by 17 P—Q R 4 if Black replied 16.., R × Kt, with some sort of a game.

(7) Simplest and best.

(8) A pretty move but quite ineffective as it finally leads to an Exchange advantageous to Black, had White moved otherwise Black would immediately have played 18.., P—B 4. The Knight cannot be taken because of 19 Q × P, Kt—B 3 ; 20 B—R 6, K—R 1 ; 21 B—Kt 5 and wins.

(9) White was threatening Kt—K 7 ch, but now all semblance of attack is over.

(10) The decisive mistake, after which White is thrown back all along the line. At any cost the Knight should have been dislodged by 22 P—Q Kt 3, Kt—Kt 3 ; 23 Q—B 3, etc., with a position less deplorable than after the text move.

(11) Much too late.

(12) Probably in order to play 28 B—Kt 3 which is now impossible on account of 27.., Kt—Q 7; 28.., Kt—B 6 ch, etc. White is completely paralysed.

(13) But this sacrifice of a Pawn is incomprehensible. Evidently better was 28 B—Kt 3 and if 28.., Kt—Q 7, then 29 B—R 2, etc.

(14) White lets his Pawns go without any struggle—the end is easily foreseen.

(15) A game well played by Rubinstein but in inferior fashion by Yates, whose combination went wrong. He did not seem to have the faculty for retrenchment, unless his somewhat reckless play was due to the score and the hope of bringing off an unexpected victory.

Game 24.   Bogoljubow *v.* Tarrasch.

Queen's Gambit Declined (in effect).

Bogoljubow	Tarrasch
1 P—Q 4	P—K 3
2 P—Q B 4	P—Q 4
3 Kt—K B 3	Kt—K B 3
4 Kt—B 3	B—K 2
5 B—Kt 5	O—O
6 P—K 3	Q Kt—Q 2
7 R—B 1	P—B 3
8 Q—B 2	P×P
9 B×P	Kt—Q 4
10 B×B (1)	Q×B
11 O—O	Kt×Kt
12 Q×Kt	P—Q Kt 3
13 Q—Q 3	R—Q 1
14 Q—K 2 (2)	P—Q B 4 (3)
15 B—Kt 5 (4)	P×P (5)
16 Kt×P	B—Kt 2 (6)
17 R—B 7	Q R—Kt 1
18 R—Q 1	B—Q 4 (7)

Bogoljubow   Tarrasch

Position after 18 R—Q 1.

19 Kt—B 6   Resigns (8)

(1) An exchange which relieves Black's cramped position. 10 B—B 4 is better—and more usual now.

(2) So far the same as the game Bogoljubow *v.* Yates. White moves out of the line of Black's Rook and with the object of B—R 6 to follow, which is prevented as things stand because of 14.., Kt—B 4.

(3) Premature and inferior to 14.., P—Q R 3 as played by Yates in the game above mentioned.

(4) Now Black has nothing better than 15.., B—Kt 2; 16 B×Kt, R×B 17 P×P, P×P; 18 Kt—K 5, R—Q 4; 19 P—B 4, Q R—Q 1, etc. with a gam^{e} perhaps defensible. His next move is a fatal error.

(5) This brings White's Knight into the game. 16 B×Kt followed by 17 P×P was threatened, still further weakening Black's game.

(6) Slightly better was 16.., Q—B 3, but the doubling of the Rooks on the Queen's Bishop's file would have settled the game in White's favour.

(7) Black has no move, *e.g.*, if 18.., Q—Kt 4 then 19 P—B 4, etc., or 18.., Q—Q 3; 19 R×B, R×R; 20 Kt—B 6, Q—B 2; 21 Kt×R, Q×Kt; 22 Q—Q 2 and wins.

(8) This evidently wins a piece and the game. Bogoljubow described his 19th move as a "family check." The shortest game of the tournament.

ROUND IX

Game 25. YATES *v.* ALEKHINE.

Ruy Lopez (Morphy Defence).

	YATES	ALEKHINE		YATES	ALEKHINE
1	P—K 4	P—K 4	32	K—B 1	K—B 2
2	Kt—K B 3	Kt—Q B 3	33	K—K 2	K—K 3
3	B—Kt 5	P—Q R 3	34	K—Q 3 (15)	R—B 4
4	B—R 4	Kt—B 3	35	R—Q Kt 4	R—Q 4 ch
5	O—O	B—B 4 (1)	36	K—K 3	R—K 4 ch
6	P—B 3 (2)	B—R 2	37	K—Q 3 (16)	R—K Kt 4
7	P—Q 4 (3)	Kt×K P	38	P—Kt 3	P—Kt 4
8	Q—K 2	P—B 4	39	P×P	P×P
9	P×P	O—O	40	R—K 4 ch	K—Q 4
10	Q Kt—Q 2	P—Q 4	41	R—K B 4	K—B 4
11	P×P e.p.	Kt×Q P	42	R—B 7	R—Kt 3
12	B—Kt 3 ch (4)	K—R 1	43	R—B 7 ch	K—Q 4
13	Kt—B 4	P—B 5 (5)	44	R—Kt 7	K—B 3
14	Q Kt—K 5	Kt×Kt	45	R—K 7	R—Kt 4
15	Kt×Kt	Q—Kt 4 (6)			Drawn
16	B—Q 2	B—R 6			
17	B—Q 5	Q R—K 1			
18	Q R—K 1	R—K 3 (7)			
19	Q—Q 3 (8)	B—K 6 (9)			

(see diagram)

	YATES	ALEKHINE
20	B×B (10)	R×Kt
21	B—B 1	B—Kt 5
22	B—B 3	K R—K 1 (11)
23	R×R	R×R
24	B×B (12)	Q×B
25	P—K R 3	Q—K 7 (13)
26	Q×Q	R×Q
27	B×P	R×Kt P
28	B×Kt	P×B
29	R—Q 1	R—Kt 3 (14)
30	R—Q 4	R—B 3
31	P—Q R 4	K—Kt 1

Position after 19 Q—Q 3.

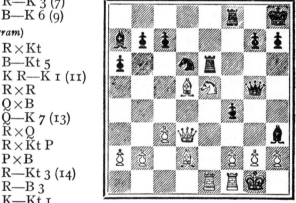

(1) This move was recommended some twenty years ago by the Danish master, Möller, but his analysis was neither thorough nor very correct. In my opinion it is due to this fact alone, that the defence has been so rarely adopted in master practice. As far as I am concerned I believe in its future and this game goes to confirm its value.

(2) Probably the best move here. If 6 Kt×P then 6.., Kt×Kt; 7 P—Q 4, Kt×P; 8 R—K 1, B—K 2; 9 R×Kt, Kt—Kt 3 with equality (Möller) or 7.., B—R 2; 8 P×Kt, Kt×P; 9 Q—Kt 4 with advantage, according to the *Handbuch*. Mr. Burn suggests 6 R—K 1, Kt—K Kt 5; 7 R—K 2 (not 7 P—Q 4, because of 7.., P×P; 8 Kt×P, Kt×Kt; 9 Q×K Kt, Castles, and Black has the better game), Kt—Q 5; 8 Kt×Kt, B×Kt; 9 P—K R 3, Kt×P. (If 9... Kt—B 3; 10 P—B 3 and 11 P—Q 4 with advantage to White); 10 R×Kt, B×R ch; 11 K×B, Q—R 5 ch; 12 K—Kt 1, Q×K P; 13 Kt—B 3 and White for preference.

(3) If 7 R—K 1 then Black obtains the advantage by the following sacrificial combinations : 7.., Kt—K Kt 5 ; 8 P—Q 4 (if 8 R—K 2, Q—B 3 ; 9 P—K R 3, P—K R 4 !, etc.). 8.., P×P ; 9 P×P (or 9 P—K R 3, K Kt—K 4 ; 10 Kt×Kt, Kt×Kt : 11 P×P, Kt—Kt 3 followed by 12.., O—O with equality), 9.., Kt×Q P ! ! ; 10 Kt×Kt, Q—R 5 ; 11 B—K 3 (if 11 Kt—B 3 then mate follows in three moves). 11.., Q×R P ch ; 12 K—B 1, Q—R 8 ch ; 13 K—K 2, Q×P, etc., with three Pawns for the piece and a very powerful attack besides.

(4) If 12 B×Kt, P×B, Black would have sufficient compensation with the two Bishops and his general attacking position for his unfavourable Pawn position.

(5) Restraining the action of the adversary's pieces whilst enlarging that of his own—the maximum that one can expect from a positional move.

(6) The signal of attack, and at the same time a defence against the threat of 16 Q—R 5, Q—B 3 ; 17 B×P, etc.

(7) A very strong move which should give Black the advantage. Not on y does it fend off the threat 19 Kt—B 7 ch but it threatens in its turn the doubling of the Rooks on the King's file with decisive pressure.

(8) The only move. If instead 19 K—R 1 then simply 19.., K R—K 1 ; 20 P×B, R×Kt and wins.

(9) An extraordinary hallucination. Feeling a bit off for play that day this move literally fascinated me ! Instead of this unsound combination I could have won a Pawn by simply playing 19.., B×P ; 20 B×B (20 P—K R 4 ?, B×R dis ch, etc.), R×Kt, etc.

(10) This move is not bad, but does not secure any advantage, whilst 20 P×B, P—B 6 ; 21 B×B P, R×B ; 22 Q—K 2 !, R×R ch ; 23 R×R would leave him with an extra Pawn. All the same it is doubtful whether this material gain would have led to victory, for after 23.., Q—K 2 ; 24 Kt—B 3 (or else 24 Q—R 5, B—B 4, etc.), B—Kt 5 and Black undoubtedly maintains the superior position.

(11) Another mistake on this occasion through pressure of time. The correct continuation was 22.., B×B ; 23 Q×B, Q—B 4 with a satisfactory game.

(12) White does likewise. 24 P—K Kt 3 would have won an important Pawn.

(13) Thus forcing an even game. Also after 25.., Q—R 5 ; 26 Q—B 3, etc., Black would not have obtained any advantage.

(14) If 29.., R×R P ; 30 R×P, P—R 3 ; 31 R—Q Kt 6, etc., with an immediate liquidation of forces.

(15) After this White has nothing further to fear and the game could now safely be abandoned as drawn.

(16) In this position White has only to avoid the exchange of Rooks. For example, 37 R—K 4, K—Q 4 ! ; 38 R×R ch, P×R ; 39 K—Q 3, P—K 5 ch winning.

Game 26.   THOMAS *v.* BOGOLJUBOW.

Ruy Lopez (Morphy Defence).

THOMAS	BOGOLJUBOW	THOMAS	BOGOLJUBOW
1 P—K 4	P—K 4	7 O—O	O—O
2 Kt—K B 3	Kt—Q B 3	8 P—Q 4	B—Q 2 (2)
3 B—Kt 5	P—Q R 3	9 B—B 2	B—Kt 5
4 B—R 4	Kt—B 3	10 R—Q 1	P×P (3)
5 Q—K 2	P—Q 3 (1)	11 P×P	Kt—Q 2
6 P—B 3	B—K 2	12 Kt—B 3	R—K 1

13 P—K 5 (4)	P—K Kt 3	31 R—K 8	Kt—Kt 4
14 P—K R 3	B × Kt	32 R—Q R 8	Kt—K 5
15 Q × B	P × P (5)	33 B—K 3	P—Kt 4
16 P × P	K Kt × P	34 R × P (15)	K—Kt 3
17 Q—B 4	B—Q 3 (6)	35 P—K Kt 3 (16)	P—R 4
18 Kt—K 4	P—B 4 (7)	36 P—Q Kt 4 (17)	K—B 2
19 B—Kt 3 ch	Kt—B 2 (8)	37 R—R 7 (18)	R × R

Position after 19 B—Kt 3 ch.

20 Kt × B	P × Kt	38 B × R	Kt—B 6
21 B—K 3 (9)	R—K 4	39 P—R 3	Kt—Kt 4
22 Q—B 4 (10)	P—Q 4 (11)	40 B—K 3	Kt × P
23 R × P	R × R	41 B × P	K—K 3 (19)
24 Q × R	Q × Q	42 K—K 2	Kt—Kt 4
25 B × Q	R—Q 1	43 K—K 3	K—K 4
26 B × Kt (12)	P × B	44 B—R 6	K—B 3
27 R—Q B 1	R—Q B 1	45 K—Q 3	Kt—B 2
28 K—B 1	K—B 1 (13)	46 B—Q 2	Kt—K 3 (20)
29 B—B 5 ch	K—Kt 2	47 B—B 3 ch	K—K 2
30 R—K 1 (14)	R—B 2	48 B—K 5	Kt—B 1
		49 K—B 4	Kt—K 3
		50 P—B 4	K—Q 2
		51 K—B 3	Kt—B 1
		52 K—Q 4	Kt—K 3 ch
		53 K—B 4	K—K 2
		54 K—Kt 3	K—Q 2
		55 K—R 4	K—B 1
		56 K—R 5	K—Kt 2
		57 P—Kt 5 (21)	Kt—B 4 (22)
		58 B—B 3	Kt—K 5
		59 B—K 1	Kt—Q 3
		60 P—Kt 6 (23)	Kt—K 5
		61 P—Kt 4	B P × P
		62 P × P	P × P
		63 P—B 5 (24)	Drawn

(1) Modern theory considers and in my opinion justly so that 5.., P—Q Kt 4 followed by 6.., B—B 4 is stronger.

(2) Threatening to gain a Pawn by 9.., P × P; 10 P × P, Kt × Q P.

(3) Abandoning the centre is a strategic error of which the consequences are soon made evident. By playing 10.., Kt—Q 2; 11 P—K R 3, B × Kt; 12 Q × B, B—Kt 4 Black obtains a satisfactory game.

(4) The beginning of a dangerous and persistent attack. Black cannot at once take the Pawn for after 13.., P × P; 14 Q—K 4, P—B 4; 15 Q—Q 5 ch, K—R 1; 16 P × P, K Kt × P; 17 Kt × Kt, Kt × Kt; 18 P—B 3, etc., he loses a piece. White is threatening B × P ch, etc., immediately.

(5) Now on the other hand the capture of the Pawn provides Black's best chance of defence.

(6) Also after 17.., Q—B 1; 18 Kt—Q 5, B—Q 1; 19 B—K 3, etc. White would have had more than an equivalent for the Pawn in this attacking position

(7) Already there is nothing better to be done. If 18.., Kt—Q 6, then simply 19 R×Kt, B×Q; 20 R×Q, Q R×R; 21 B×B, etc., with a Piece to the good.

(8) If 19.., K—R 1; 20 Kt—Kt 5 (threatening 21 Kt×P), Q—K 2; 21 Q—K R 4 with the threat of B—B 7.

Mr. Burn suggests however, if 19.., K—R 1; 20 Kt×B, P×Kt; 21 Q—R 6 with 22 B—Kt 5 to follow leaving Black in a very unenviable position, but Mr. Alekhine's suggestion is the more convincing.

(9) It is not evident why White refrains from retaking the Pawn at once, for after 21 R×P, R—K 8 ch; 22 K—R 2, Q—K 2 (or K 1); 23 Q—Kt 3 with the threat of 24 B—R 6 Black would have no satisfactory defence. As played the result of the game would have been doubtful had Black played 21.. Kt—K 4.

(10) This regains the Pawn all the same and White gets a very advantageous end-game.

(11) If 22.., Q—K 2; 23 R×P, Q×R; 24 Q×Kt ch, K—R 1; 25 B—R 6 with mate inevitable.

(12) White sacrifices one advantage—that of his two Bishops against the two Knights—to gain another and one which will soon become decisive, *i.e.,* the weakening of Black's Queen's side Pawns.

(13) The decisive error after which Black will no longer be able to defend the Queen's Rook's Pawn. The best defensive reply was 28.., Kt—K 4 followed by 29.., K—B 2. It is hardly necessary to add that in this case White would have retained considerable chance of winning.

(14) Prevents Black's 30.., Kt—K 4 and threatens 31 R—K 7 and 32 R—R 7, etc., against which Black had no satisfactory guard.

(15) With a passed Pawn to the good and a position much superior a win for White is only a matter of technique.

(16) He could also play at once 35 P—Q R 4, etc.

(17) Certainly superior and more direct would have been 36 P—Q R 4. At the same time the text move loses nothing—it even threatens to win another Pawn by 37 P—Kt 5.

(18) A singular error of judgment by which White draws a game otherwise easily won. The proper line was 37 P—Q R 4, 38 P—R 5 and 39 R—R 8, 40 P—R 6, etc. If 37 P—Q R 4, R—Kt 2 naturally 38 B—Kt 6. The text move not only forces an exchange entirely to Black's advantage but also allows him to exchange his Knight's Pawn for the dangerous passed Pawn. Now with a correct defence Black manages to draw.

(19) Not the best move. This creates some technical difficulties for Black The correct plan of defence is to place the Knight on K 3, so the King should not have occupied this square. Fortunately for himself Black notices his mistake in time and can still retrieve.

(20) This makes the draw certain.

(21) A last effort.

(22) The entrance of the Knight destroys White's last hope of a win, who sees himself obliged to defend his King's Knight's Pawn.

(23) After 60 P×P ch, K×P, etc., Black would have some chance of victory.

(24) Black cannot advance the Knight's Pawn for after 63.., P—Kt 6; 64 B×P, Kt×B; 65 P—B 6, there would be no stopping the White Pawn, so there is nothing for it but a draw.

Game 27.   TARRASCH *v.* RUBINSTEIN.

Four Knights' Game (*Double Ruy Lopez*).

	TARRASCH	RUBINSTEIN		TARRASCH	RUBINSTEIN
1	P—K 4	P—K 4	40	R—Q 2 ch	K—B 2
2	Kt—K B 3	Kt—Q B 3	41	R—K 2	R—R 2
3	Kt—B 3	Kt—B 3	42	R—K 6	R—B 2
4	B—Kt 5	B—Kt 5	43	R—K 3	B—Q 2
5	O—O	O—O	44	K—B 2	R—R 2
6	B×Kt	Q P×B	45	K—Kt 1	K—Q 1 (15)
7	Kt×P (1)	R—K 1	46	R—K 1	R—K 2
8	Kt—Q 3	B×Kt	47	R×R (16)	K×R
9	Q P×B	Kt×P	48	K—B 2	K—K 3
10	Q—B 3	Kt—Q 3	49	P—Kt 3	B—B 3
11	B—B 4	Q—B 3	50	K—K 2	K—B 2
12	K R—K 1	B—K 3	51	K—K 3	P—B 4
13	Q—Kt 3	B—Q 4	52	K—K 2	B—Q 2
14	Q—Kt 5 (2)	Q×Q	53	K—K 3	K—Kt 3
15	B×Q	P—Q R 4 (3)	54	K—K 2	K—R 4
16	P—Q R 3	P—B 3	55	K—K 3	B—K 1
17	B—B 4	K—B 2	56	K—B 2	P—B 5
18	P—B 3	P—Q Kt 3 (4)	57	P×P	P×P
19	R×R	R×R	58	K—Kt 2	K—R 5
20	R—K 1	R—Q 1 (5)	59	K—R 2	B—Q 2
21	K—B 2	P—K Kt 4	60	K—Kt 2	B—B 3
22	B—Kt 3 (6)	B—K 3	61	K—B 2 (17)	
23	P—K R 4	P—R 3		Drawn	
24	P×P	R P×P			
25	P—R 4 (7)	P—Q B 4			
26	K—B 1 (8)	B—B 4			
27	R—K 2	B—Q 2 (9)			
28	P—Kt 3	P—B 5			
29	Kt—Kt 2 (10)	B—K 3			
30	B×Kt (11)	R×B			
31	P×P (12)	P—Q B 4 (13)			
32	K—K 1	B—Q 2			
33	K—B 2	B—B 3			
34	K—B 1	R—Q 2			
35	K—B 2	R—Q 1			
36	K—B 1	R—K R 1			
37	K—Kt 1 (14)	R—R 5			
	(*see diagram*)				
38	R—Q 2	K—K 2			
39	R—K 2 ch	K—Q 2			

Position after 37 K—Kt 1.

(1) With this somewhat unusual capture White seems to be playing for a draw in getting a symmetrical Pawn position and with Bishops of opposite colour. It is very instructive to see by what follows how Rubinstein succeeds in combating this tendency.

(2) Now that Queen's must also be exchanged what can happen ?

(3) A first attempt to break the symmetry to which White should have replied by 16 P—Q R 4 followed by 17 P—Q Kt 3 and 18 P—Q B 4, etc. Instead of that he begins to make faulty moves which might have resulted in disaster.

(4) So that he can reply to 19 P—Q Kt 3 with 19.., P—Q B 4 followed by 20.., P—B 5, etc. Black has already a slight advantage.

(5) It is clear that exchange of Rooks in this position will destroy all hope of winning.

(6) Slightly better would be 22 B—B 1, although in this case also Black retains after 22.., P—Q B 4 the initiative on the Queen's side.

(7) Too late, as Black's reply proves. But if White had played a waiting game Black could at any time have reinforced his position, and threatened with R—Q 2 followed by B—B 4 and Kt—B 5 or if need were P—Q B 4, etc.

(8) Plainly White no longer knows quite what to do.

(9) Produces fresh weaknesses in White's game.

(10) The decisive mistake—for it is not evident how Black after 29 Kt—B 1 could, in spite of his clear superiority of position, have forced the enemy's stronghold. As it is the White Knight will remain in a tragi-comic situation to the end of the game.

(11) There is nothing better, for after 30 P—Kt 4, P×P ; 31 P×P, P—B 6 ; 32 Kt—Q 3, R—Q R 1, White would lose a Pawn immediately.

(12) After 31 Kt×P, B×Kt ; 32 P×B, R—Q 8 ch ; 33 K—B 2 (or else 33 R—K 1, R×R ch with a winning Pawn end-game) ; 33.., R—Q R 8 the end-game would have been easily won by Black.

(13) The winning position is achieved. It is now only a question of winning it and here Black goes astray.

(14) The idea for winning in this position is as follows : It will be seen as the game proceeds that Black cannot win if he exchanges Rooks, without altering the present combination of Pawns on the King's side, for in that case his King will not be able to play his part, whereas if he exchanges his King's Knight's Pawn for White's King's Bishop's Pawn and after that forces the exchange of Rooks, the Black Bishop's Pawn advancing would have been able finally to seize White's Knight's Pawn on account of White's lack of moves. The position obtained on the 37th move was precisely what was needed for the realisation of this plan, *e.g.*, 37.., P—Kt 5 ; 38 P—B 4 (or else 38 P×P, R—K Kt 1, etc.), 38.., P—Kt 6 ; 39 R—K 3, R—R 5 ; 40 P—B 5, R—R 4 ; 41 R×P, R×P ; 42 R—Kt 4, R—K 4 ; 43 K—B 2, R—K 1 ; 44 R—Kt 3, R—Q 1 ; 45 R—Q 3, R—K Kt 1 ; 46 R—Kt 3 (or 46 P—Kt 3, R—K R 1), 46.., R×R ; 47 K×R, K—K 3 ; 48 K—B 2, K—B 4 ; 49 K—Kt 3, K—Kt 4 ; 50 K—B 2, K—Kt 5, etc., wins. Of course Rubinstein might still in the following moves have adopted the same plan, but he does not seem to have thought about it at all.

(15) Here again 45.., P—Kt 5 was well worth looking at. Instead of that Black aims at the exchange of Rooks.

(16) Now the game is drawn.

(17) Black, after the exchange of Rooks, has obtained the maximum reinforcement of his position and is only at this stage convinced that to win is no longer possible, *e.g.*, 61.., K—R 6 ; 62 Kt—Q 3 (at last), B× RP ; 63 Kt×P ch, K—R 5 ; 64 Kt—Q 5, B×P ; 65 Kt×P, P—R 5 ; 66 Kt×P, B×Kt ; 67 K—K 3, B—Kt 6 ; 68 K—K 4, B×P ; 69 K—K 5, B moves ; 70 P—Q B 4, followed by 71 K—Q 6.

ROUND X

Game 28.   BOGOLJUBOW *v.* ALEKHINE.
Queen's Pawn Opening (Dutch Defence).

	BOGOLJUBOW	ALEKHINE		BOGOLJUBOW	ALEKHINE
1	P—Q 4	P—K B 4 (1)	36	R—Q Kt 8	B—Kt 4
2	P—Q B 4	Kt—K B 3	37	R × B	Q × R
3	P—K Kt 3	P—K 3	38	P—Kt 4 (29)	Kt—B 6 ch
4	B—Kt 2 (2)	B—Kt 5 ch	39	B × Kt	P × B
5	B—Q 2	B × B ch	40	P × P (30)	Q—K 7 (31)
6	Kt × B (3)	Kt—B 3	41	P—Q 5	K—Kt 1 (32)
7	K Kt—B 3	O—O	42	P—R 5	K—R 2
8	O—O	P—Q 3	43	P—K 4	Kt × K P
9	Q—Kt 3 (4)	K—R 1	44	Kt × Kt	Q × Kt
10	Q—B 3	P—K 4 (5)	45	P—Q 6 (33)	P × P
11	P—K 3	P—Q R 4 (6)	46	P—B 6	P × P
12	P—Kt 3 (7)	Q—K 1	47	R—Q 2	Q—K 7 (34)
13	P—Q R 3	Q—R 4 (8)	48	R × Q	P × R
14	P—K R 4 (9)	Kt—K Kt 5	49	K—B 2	P × Kt (Q) ch
15	Kt—Kt 5 (10)	B—Q 2	50	K × Q	K—Kt 2
16	P—B 3 (11)	Kt—B 3	51	K—K 2	K—B 2
17	P—B 4 (12)	P—K 5	52	K—K 3	K—K 3
18	K R—Q 1 (13)	P—R 3	53	K—K 4	P—Q 4 ch
19	Kt—R 3	P—Q 4 (14)		Resigns	
20	Kt—B 1	Kt—K 2 (15)			
21	P—R 4	Kt—B 3 (16)			
22	R—Q 2	Kt—Q Kt 5			
23	B—R 1 (17)	Q—K 1 (18)			
24	R—K Kt 2 (19)	P × P			
25	P × P	B × P			
26	Kt—B 2	B—Q 2			
27	Kt—Q 2	P—Q Kt 4 (20)			
28	Kt—Q 1	Kt—Q 6 (21)			
29	R × P (22)	P—Kt 5			
30	R × R (23)	P × Q (24)			

(*see diagram*).

31	R × Q	P—B 7 (25)	
32	R × R ch	K—R 2 (26)	
33	Kt—B 2	P—B 8 (Q) ch	
34	Kt—B 1	Kt—K 8 (27)	
35	R—R 2	Q × B P (28)	

Position after 30 R × R.

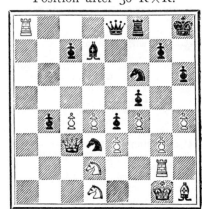

(1) A risky defence, which up to the present I have only on very rare occasions adopted in serious encounters. Its repute appears to be, however, much worse than its actual merit.

(2) This fianchetto development evolved by Steinitz and adopted later by Rubinstein does not appear to be the best line of attack; Black with the succeeding move obtains at least equality.

(3) 6 Q × B, followed by 7 Kt—Q B 3 is possibly preferable.

(4) This move does not in any way hamper Black's plans; it is, however, difficult to suggest an alternative and efficacious continuation for White.

(5) This advance is feasible, as after the Exchanges in the centre the Queen's Knight is attacked by the Black Queen.

(6) As will be seen, it was most important to prevent for the moment P—Q Kt 4.

(7) Not 12 P—Q R 3 on account of 12.., P—R 5.

(8) By this move Black obtains an attacking position. White cannot play 14 P×P, P×P ; 15 Kt×P, Kt×Kt ; 16 Q×Kt on account of 16.., Kt—Kt 5, winning. Nor can White play 14 P—Q Kt 4 on account of 14.., P—K 5 ; 15 Kt—K 1, P×P, etc.

(9) A good move which secures a new retreat for the King's Knight and renews the threat of P×P.

(10) White wants to get rid of the menacing Knight as quickly as possible.

(11) If 16 B×Kt, B×B ; 17 P—B 3 then 17.., P×P ; 18 P×Kt, P×Q ; 19 P×Q, P×Kt, etc., with far the superior end-game.

(12) Already necessary in view of the threat of 17.., P—B 5, etc.

(13) In order to protect the King's Knight's Pawn now threatened by Q—Kt 5, followed by Kt—R 4.

(14) By this move Black completely destroys White's hopes in the centre and soon obtains in an unexpected manner the initiative on the Queen's side.

(15) Preparing for P—R 5 !

(16) Now instead the Knight can enter the adversary's game *via* Q Kt 5 and Q 6, etc.

(17) A complicated manoeuvre which has for its object an attack on the King's side, clearly pointing to White's inferiority.

(18) This powerful move gives Black in every possible way a fresh advantage. If 24 P×P then the command of the square Q 4, or else if 24 P—B 5 the command of an open file by 24.., P—Q Kt 4 ! or as the game actually proceeded the gain of a Pawn.

(19) Still trying to advance P—K Kt 4, but even this is not conceded.

(20) The renewal of the struggle for the centre square. A fight in which the crisis concludes with a stirring and original finish.

(21) This move prepares the combination which follows ; very much weaker would have been 28.., P×P, as the White Knight would eventually have found a good square on K 5.

(22) If 29 P×P, B×P ; 30 R×P, Kt—Q 4 ; 31 Q—R 3, R×R ; 32 Q×R, Q—B 3, with a winning attack.

(23) Or else 30 Q—R1, R×R ; 31 Q×R, Q—R 1 ! ; 32 Q×Q, R×Q, and the entry of the Rook into the game clinches matters.

(24) As will be seen this is far superior to 30.., Q×R ; 31 Q—Kt 3, B—R 5 ; 32 Q—Kt 1 and White can still defend himself.

(25) The point of the combination.

(26) Evidently the only move.

(27) Threatening mate.

(28) Again threatening mate by 36.., B—Kt 4 ; 37 Kt—Q 2, Q—B 8, etc., thus forcing White to sacrifice the Exchange.

(29) The only way to prolong the game, but at the same time allowing another surprise.

(30) Forced ; for if 40 P—Kt 5 Black obtains two passed Pawns by 40.., Kt—Kt 5, etc.

(31) This move produces a problematical position in which no piece can move without immediate loss ; for example, 41 Kt—R 3 (or K 4) ; Kt—Kt 5 ! ! ; or 41 R—R 3 (or R 1), Kt—Kt 5 and wins in each case. Thus after two meaningless Pawn moves White must play 43 P—K 4 which brings the position to an immediate liquidation of forces with a won Pawn end-game.

(32) And not the plausible 41.., P—R 4, as White would then be able to save himself by 42 Kt—R 3, and if 42.., Kt—Kt 5, 43 Kt—Kt 5 ch, K moves ; 44 R×Q, P×R ; 45 Kt—B 3, etc.

(33) So as to dislocate Black's Pawns as White cannot defend his.

(34) A pretty ending well in keeping with this fine game, Black now forces won Pawn ending.

Game 29.   RUBINSTEIN *v.* THOMAS.
Queen's Pawn Opening.

RUBINSTEIN	THOMAS	RUBINSTEIN	THOMAS
1 P—Q 4	Kt—K B 3	47 R—Kt 2	K—B 1
2 P—Q B 4	P—K Kt 3 (1)	48 R—Kt 1	K—B 2 1
3 Kt—Q B 3	B—Kt 2	49 R—K B 1	K—Kt
4 P—K Kt 3 (2)	P—Q 3	50 Q—B 2	Q—B 2
5 B—Kt 2	O—O	51 Q×R P	R—B 1
6 P—K 4	P—K 4	52 Q—Kt 5	K—R 2
7 K Kt—K 2	Kt—B 3 (3)	53 K—R 4	K—Kt 1
8 O—O	R—K 1	54 R—K Kt 1	K—R 2
9 P—Q 5	Kt—Kt 1 (4)	55 R—Kt 3	R—B 1
10 P—B 3 (5)	Q Kt—Q 2	56 K—R 3	R—B 1
11 B—K 3	P—K R 3	57 K—R 4	R—B 1
12 P—Q Kt 4 (6)	P—Kt 3	58 R—Kt 2	R—Q Kt 1 (21)
13 Kt—R 4	P—Q R 4 (7)	59 R—K B 2	R—K B 1
14 P—Q R 3	P×P	60 R—B 1	K—R 1
15 P×P	B—Kt 2	61 Kt—B 3	Q—K 1
16 K Kt—B 3	Q—K 2 (8)	62 Kt—Kt 5	Q—B 2
17 Kt—Kt 5	K R—Q B 1	63 Q—R 6 ch	K—Kt 1
18 B—R 3	Kt—K 1	64 R—K Kt 1	Q—K 2 ch (22)
19 Q—Q 2	K—R 2	65 K—Kt 3	R—B 3
20 Q Kt—B 3 (9)	K R—Kt 1	66 Q—Kt 5	Q—B 2
21 Kt—R 7	Q Kt—B 3	67 Q—K 3	R—Kt 3 ch
22 R—R 3	Kt—Kt 1 (10)	68 K—B 2	R×R
23 K R—R 1	B—K B 1	69 K×R (23)	Kt—K 1
24 P—Kt 5 (11)	Kt—Kt 2	70 K—B 2	K—R 2
25 Kt—B 6	B×Kt	71 K—Kt 3	Q—Kt 3 ch
26 Kt P×B	Q—Q 1	72 K—R 3	Q—B 3
27 Kt—Kt 5	Kt—K 1	73 K—Kt 3	Q—Kt 3 ch
28 Q—R 2	R×R	74 K—R 3	Q—B 3
29 Q×R	P—R 4 (12)	75 Kt—B 3 (24)	Kt—Kt 2
30 Q—R 7	B—R 3	76 Kt—K 2	Q—Kt 3
31 B×B	K×B	77 Kt—B 1	K—Kt 1
32 B—Q 7 (13)	Q Kt—B 3	78 Kt—Q 3	K—R 2
33 K—B 2 (14)	P—Kt 4		
34 K—Kt 2 (15)	K—Kt 2		
35 B—B 5	K—B 1		

(see diagram)

RUBINSTEIN	THOMAS
36 P—R 4 (16)	P×P
37 P×P	Kt—Kt 1
38 K—Kt 3 (17)	Kt—K 2
39 Kt—B 3 (18)	Kt—Kt 3 (19)
40 B×Kt	P×B
41 Q—R 3	P—K Kt 4
42 Q—B 1	P×P ch
43 K—R 3 (20)	Q—B 3
44 Q—K 3	Kt—Kt 2
45 Kt—Kt 5	R—B 1
46 R—K Kt 1	K—B 2

Position after 35.., K—B 1.

79	Kt—K 1	Q—B 3	
80	Kt—Kt 2	Q—Kt 3	
81	Kt—R 4	Q—B 3	
82	Q—B 1 (25)	K—Kt 1	
83	Q—Kt 2	K—R 2	
84	Q—Kt 2	K—R 3	
85	Q—Kt 3	K—R 2	
86	Q—Kt 1	K—R 3	
87	Q—Kt 1(26)	K—R 2	
88	Q—Q B 1	K—Kt 1	
89	K—Kt 3	K—R 2	
90	P—B 4	P×P ch	
91	Q×P	Q—K 2	
92	Kt—B 3	K—Kt 3 (27)	
93	K—B 2	Q—B 3	
94	Q—Kt 3 ch	K—R 3	
95	Q—R 3 (28)	Q—B 5	
96	P—K 5 (29)	Kt—B 4	
97	P—K 6	K—Kt 3	
98	Q—R 1	Q—K 6 ch (30)	
99	K—Kt 2	Q—K 7 ch	
100	K—R 3	Q—K B 7 (31)	
101	Q—Kt 2 ch	Q×Q ch	
102	K×Q	Kt—K 6 ch	
103	K—B 2	Kt×B P	
104	Kt—Q 4	Kt—R 6	
105	K—K 2	K—B 3 (32)	
106	K—Q 3	P—R 5	
107	Kt—B 5	P—R 6	
108	Kt×P (33)	P—R 7	
109	Kt—K 4 ch	K—K 2	
110	P—Q 6 ch (34)	P×P	
111	P—B 7	P—R 8 (Q)	
112	P—B 8 (Q)	Q—B 6 ch	
113	K—Q 2 (35)	Q—B 5 ch(36)	
114	K—Q 3	Drawn	

(1) This is the fashionable variation. In my encounter with Reti in London in 1922. the continuing moves were 3 Kt—Q B 3, B—Kt 2 ; 4 Kt—B 3, O—O ; 5 P—K 4, etc., and I, playing White, obtained much the superior game.

(2) This is Rubinstein's favourite development played in all similar openings. In the present game he was not, as it turned out, to obtain any marked advantage.

(3) To have obtained such a simple and effective development from an irregular start makes one doubt whether White's plan was really irreproachable.

(4) Mr. Burn thinks Black's error was his 8th move and suggests instead 8.., P×P; 9 Kt×P, Kt×P; 10 Kt×Q Kt, Kt×Kt; 11 Kt×Q, Kt×Q; 12 Kt×Kt P, R—Kt 1 ; 13 R×Kt, B×Kt; 14 R—Kt 1, B×B; 15 K×B, K R—K 1 and equality. In my opinion this retreat (9.., Kt—Kt 1) is clearly at fault and puts Black into a very difficult position. The natural move was 9.., Kt—Q 5, forcing the exchange of minor pieces with a satisfactory game. White takes advantage of this mistake in masterly fashion.

(5) A master stroke, by which White prepares for the advance on the Queen's side. The Bishop when on K 3 must not be subject to the threat of exchange by Kt—Kt 5.

(6) From here up to the won position on move 35 White plays correctly. The game affords a typical example of a Queen's side attack in a blocked position.

(7) The opening of the Rook's file, as it will be seen, is entirely to White's advantage, but the threatened 14 P—B 5 was very disagreeable.

(8) Just in time ! Had he delayed this move now he could never have freed the Queen.

(9) The prime object of White's play is to get possession of the open file, by doubling the Rooks after Kt—R 7. Black cannot counter by exchanging Rooks for after 20.., R×R ; 21 R×R, R—R 1 ; 22 R×R, B×R, the manoeuvre Q—R 2 and R 7 wins at once.

(10) Black has no satisfactory move. The game is strategically lost.

(11) This is the initial move of a decisive manoeuvre. After the exchange at B 6 and of a Rook, White will be able to attack the weak Pawn at Q B 7 in superior force. This should have been the end.

(12) Black at last makes an attempt to exchange at least one of his inactive pieces, but it is much too late.

(13) 32 Q—Kt 7 would be premature in view of 32.., P—B 4, etc.

(14) The Bishop cannot be taken on account of 33.., Kt×B; 34 P×Kt, Kt—B 3 ; 35 Q×B P, Q×Q; 36 Kt×Q, Kt×P (Q 7); 36 Kt—Kt 5 with a won end-game. Otherwise White threatens 34 P—R 3 followed by 35 P—Kt 4, P×P ; 36 R P×P, etc., leading to the shifting of the Black Knight, after which

Q—Kt 7 and R—R 7 win off-hand. Conscious of the danger Black makes a move of despair.

(15) An unnecessary refinement; 34 B—B 5 followed by 35 Q—Kt 7, etc., was immediately decisive.

(16) As Rubinstein himself demonstrates, he could have finished the game, played in a masterly fashion to this point, by the evident 36 Q—Kt 7 followed by 37 R—R 7, or if Black takes the Queen, by 37 P × R and 38 B—B 8, etc. The text-move is very weak, as it gives Black for no reason at all something to play for on the King's side, after which the game can only be won with great difficulty, or perhaps not at all.

(17) The first defensive move. 38 Q—Kt 7 would have been insufficient on account of 38.., Kt—K 2 followed by 39.., Kt—Kt 3, etc.

(18) The beginning of a retreat all along the line which, had it been effected in time would still have left White with a superior game.

(19) Not 39.., Kt × B; 40 P × Kt, Kt—Kt 2; 41 P—B 6, Kt—B 4 ch; 42 K—B 2, etc., winning.

(20) The Pawn is only surrendered temporarily, as evidently White quickly recovers it with the Queen. White's winning chance now consists in the fact that in most lines of play he can invite exchange of Queens with a won end-game. Black has a very difficult game to play,and his method of conducting it merits only praise.

(21) A move which clearly demonstrates to White that Black sees the result of playing 58.., R—Q R 1 and that he does not intend risking it. The threat was if 58.., R—Q R 1; 59 Q × Kt ch, Q × Q; 60 R × Q ch, K × R; 61 Kt × B P and as the Rook is now attacked White has the necessary time to win the Queen's Pawn with a decisive advantage.

(22) This move brings about a sensible improvement in Black's position. He now effects exchange of Rooks.

(23) After this Exchange surely White's chances are not increased. White's only hope now lies in P—B 4, which he does twenty moves later, and even so it tends to a weakening of his position.

(24) This Knight now leaves the post he has held off and on for nearly fifty moves in order to help on the King's side.

(25) Preparing for the advance of the King's Bishop's Pawn, which he does not finally decide upon for another eight moves.

(26) White plays to induce the likely looking move 87.., Q—Kt 4, whereupon he would play 88 P—B 5, with good winning chances, but Black has an eye for everything.

(27) The only, but a sufficient defence against the threatened 93 P—K 5. This would now be met by 93.., Kt—B 4 ch; 94 K—B 2, P × P; 95 Kt × P ch, K—B 3; 96 Kt—Q 7 ch, K—Kt 3, and White would have no chance of winning.

(28) The beginning of a dangerous manoeuvre whereby White risks losing the game.

(29) The logical outcome of his last move. If 96 Q—Q 7, Q × P; 97 Q × P, Kt—B 4; 98 Q × P, Q—B 7 ch; 99 K—Kt 1, Q × P and draws. (Mr. Burn, in *The Field*, points out that this suggested variation is faulty and 97.., Kt—B 4 loses as follows: 98 Q—R 7 ch, K × Q; 99 Kt—Kt 5 ch, K moves; 100 Kt × Q and wins).

(30) White has reduced himself to the defensive. It is not obvious what he would have done had Black taken the Pawn with Queen, *e.g.*, 98.., Q × P; 99 Q—Kt 1 ch, Q—Kt 5, or 99 Q—Kt 1, Q—B 5, etc., with all the threats of the text retained with a Pawn plus.

(31) White now has a lost game. Black could have won here by 100.., Q × B P; 101 Q—Kt 2 ch, Q—Kt 5 ch; 102 Q × Q ch, P × Q ch; 103 K × P, Kt—K 6 ch; 104 K—B 4, Kt × P ch and wins. The text-move allows White to draw.

(32) 105.., P—R 5 is certainly better, but doubtful whether it forces a win.

(33) In spite of his ingenuity White is unable to get a win out of such a sterile position.

(34) The ending is very piquant and compensates for the tedium of the preceding fifty-nine moves.

(35) This is forced as otherwise if 113 K—Q 4, Kt—Kt 4 ch; 114 K—B 4, Q × Kt ch; 115 K × Kt, Q × P; 116 Q—B 7 ch, Q—Q 2 ch winning.

(36) It is evident that Black, if he plays 113.., Q × Kt would be forced to draw after 114 Q—Q 7 ch, K—B 3; 115 Q—B 7 ch, K moves; 116 P—K 7.

Game 30.   YATES *v.* TARRASCH.

French Defence (McCutcheon Defence).

YATES	TARRASCH	YATES	TARRASCH
1 P—K 4	P—K 3	27 Q R—B 1	K R—B 1
2 P—Q 4	P—Q 4	28 R—K 3	Q—Q 2 (13)
3 Kt—Q B 3	Kt—K B 3	29 P—B 4	B—B 1
4 B—Kt 5	B—Kt 5	30 P—B 5	P×P
5 P—K 5	P—K R 3	31 R×P	Kt—R 3 (14)
6 B—Q 2	B×Kt	32 R×B	R×R
7 P×B	Kt—K 5	33 Q×Kt	R—B 7
8 Q—Kt 4	K—B 1 (1)	34 B—R 3 (15)	R×P
9 B—B 1 (2)	P—Q B 4 (3)	35 R—Q B 3 (16)	R—Q Kt 1
10 B—Q 3	Kt×Q B P (4)	36 P—R 3	K R—Kt 7
11 P×P (5)	Q—R 4	37 R—K Kt 3	Q—Q B 2 (17)
12 B—Q 2	Q×B P	38 Kt—B 4	R—Kt 8 ch
13 Kt—K 2	Kt—K 5 (6)	39 K—R 2	Q R—R 8
14 B×Kt	P×B	40 R—Q 3	Q—B 2 (18)
15 Q×P (K 4)	Kt—B 3	41 Kt—Q 2	R—Kt 8 (19)
16 B—B 3	P—Q Kt 3	42 Q—B 6	Q—Kt 3
17 O—O	B—R 3 (7)	43 P—Kt 3 (20)	Q—R 4
18 B—Kt 2	Q—Q 4 (8)	44 P—Kt 4 (21)	Q—R 5
19 Q—K 3	Q—Kt 4 (9)	45 B—B 5	Q—K 8
		46 Q—B 3	R—R 8 ch (22)

Position after 19 Q—K 3.

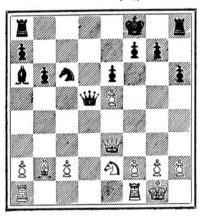

Position after 46 Q—B 3.

20 Q—R 3 ch	K—Kt 1		
21 Kt—Kt 3	K—R 2		
22 K R—K 1	Q R—Q 1 (10)	47 K—Kt 2	R—Kt 8 ch
23 Q R—Kt 1	Q—B 5	48 K—R 2	R—R 8 ch
24 Kt—K 4	Kt—Kt 1 (11)	49 K—Kt 2	R—Kt 8 ch
25 Kt—Q 6	Q—B 2	50 K—R 2	R—R 8 ch
26 P—Q B 4	P—B 4 (12)		Drawn

(1) This defensive move is much stronger than 8.., P—K Kt 3 on which White would be able to institute a strong attack by 9 P—K R 4, whereas Black now can reply with advantage to this move with 9.., Kt—Q B 3, 10.., Kt—K 2; 11.., Kt—K B 4, etc.

(2) A Pawn sacrifice to obtain valuable time and retain the Queen's Bishop. Black is right to refuse it.

(3) It is important to make this move, which begins an initiative on the Queen's side before White checks at Q R 3.

(4) Now the capture of the Pawn leads, after a few forced moves, to a position definitely in favour of Black.

(5) If 11 B—R 3, then 11.., Kt—Q 2; 12 P×P, Kt×K P; 13 P—B 6 ch, K—Kt 1 with advantage.

(6) The only move in view of the eventual B—Kt 4, but it is quite sufficient.

(7) It is plain that Black's initiative persists. White's Pawns are weak and his pieces badly placed.

(8) A very good move, for after 19 Q×Q, P×Q; 20 K R—K 1, B×Kt; 21 R×B, K—K 2, Black would have a much superior end-game.

(9) This is the first crisis in the game. Instead of continuing with 19.. Kt—R 4 and if 20 K R—Q 1 then 20.., Kt—B 5; 21 R×Q, Kt×Q; 22 R—Q 7, K—K 1, etc., which increases his advantage, Black starts on a line which merely results in posting White's Knight on Q 6 where it dominates the whole game. The situation is now completely changed in a few moves.

(10) The Rook cannot be brought into play with advantage on account of the eventual attack, Kt—R 5 followed by Q—K Kt 3, etc.

(11) Practically forced in view of the threat 25 Kt—Q 6. Still worse would be 24.., Kt—R 4 on account of 25 Q—K B 3, etc.

(12) A good move, at least allowing a satisfactory defence on the King's side, but all the same Black's position remains very precarious.

(13) In order to free his Bishop, at present impossible on account of 29 Kt—Kt 5.

(14) The sacrifice of two pieces for the Rook offers the best chance for 31.., Kt—B 3 leads to a *débâcle* after 32 K R—Q B 3.

(15) The second crisis. 34 R—K 2, K R—B 1; 35 P—K R 3 or 34.., Q—Q B 2; 35 B—Q 4, etc., provides a sufficient defence and probable victory, but now Black again gets the advantage.

(16) 35 P—R 3 at once was probably better, although in this case also the doubling of the Rooks on the 7th or 8th rank would have been very unpleasant for White.

(17) A good attacking move for Black. The reply 38 Kt—K 8 would be met by 38.., Q—B 8 ch; 39 K—R 2, Q×P, etc.

(18) Dr. Tarrasch conducts the attack in an irreproachable manner. Against the entry of the Queen on the King's side White has no longer any efficient defence.

(19) Much better than check for it prevents the flight of the White Queen to the centre, a retreat which might have prolonged the game.

(20) All White's moves are forced.

(21) If 44 Q—K B 3 then 44.., R—R 8 ch; 45 Q×R, R×Q ch; 46 K×R, Q—Q 8 ch; 47 K—Kt 2, Q—K 7 ch and wins.

(22) Black, very short of time, forces the draw by perpetual check, while the simple move 46.., R—Kt 6, etc., wins at once. This half point cost Dr. Tarrasch the share of a prize.